"I met Jim in 2002 in Jaraba(... we know how much we woul... ... missionary experiences. Jim and Mary taught us to give unconditionally.

"*Faith Journeys* will make you laugh and maybe cry, but foremost, it will challenge your relationship with the Lord and how to not be afraid when facing seemingly impossible situations."

Ivan Rosalia, Netherland Antilles, Literacy Evangelism International
Jarabacoa, Dominican Republic

"This book will reshape your view of what it means to be obedient to the Lord. It will call you for your response to the Great Commission. Those who seek adventure need to read this book and learn from Jim and Mary Nipp. From Indiana to Africa and beyond, north, south, east, and west, we can see how the Lord called Jim and Mary and how they followed that call, making a difference for the Lord.

"Your faith will be inspired as you read the real-life account of ones who took God's call personally and responded obediently by going into all the world."

Dr. Donna Thomas, President, Christian Vision Ministries
Carmel, Indiana

"Jim has crafted his storytelling to be inspirational and faith building. His unique way of retelling events and experiences from years past make them seem as if they had just happened the day before. Jim's stories make the promises of the Bible come alive. It is encouraging to hear how God is continuing to work miracles in people's lives today, people I personally know."

Bob Lines, Pastor, Friends Church
Kennard, Indiana

"This book was so interesting and exciting I could hardly lay it down. My faith was increased. How beautiful are the feet of those who share the gospel, which brings glad tidings of such faith, from so many conflicts, by obeying the Holy Spirit.

"With God's strength behind you and his arms beneath you, you have faced whatever was ahead of you. Continuing blessings to both you and Mary as you travel in the pathway of God."

Doris Armstrong, Christian Women's Connection
South Memorial Drive Church of God,
New Castle, Indiana

FAITH
Journeys

Faith Journeys

Stories To Inspire Your Faith
"Since my youth, God, you have taught me,
and to this day I declare your marvelous deeds.
Even when I am old and gray,
do not forsake me, my God,
till I declare your power to the next generation,
your mighty acts to all who are to come." Psalm 71:17–18

ALL RIGHTS RESERVED. No part of this work covered by the copyright hereon may be reproduced, transcribed, or used in any form or by any means—graphic, electronic, or mechanical, including photocopying, recording, taping, Web distribution, or information and retrieval systems—without permission.

All Scripture quotations, unless otherwise indicated, are taken from THE HOLY BIBLE, NEW INTERNATIONAL VERSION®, NIV® Copyright © 1973, 1978, 1984, 2011 by Biblica, Inc.™ Used by permission. All rights reserved worldwide. Scripture quotations marked "NKJV" are taken from the New King James Version. Copyright © 1982 by Thomas Nelson, Inc. Used by permission. All rights reserved. Scripture quotations marked "NIrV" are taken from the *Holy Bible, New International Reader's Version*®. *NIrV*®. Copyright ©1973, 1978, 1984 by International Bible Society. Used by permission of Zondervan. All rights reserved. Quotations marked "NKJV" are taken from the New King James Version. Copyright ©1982 by Thomas Nelson, Inc. Used by permission. All rights reserved. Quotations marked "KJV" are taken from the King James Version.

Cover photo: The Land Rover and trailer used on "the road south" to Botswana.

Printed in the United States of America

For permission to use material, contact:

James E. Nipp
World Missionary Association
P.O. Box 304
New Castle, Indiana 47362
765-524-4334
Email wmamissions@yahoo.com

Copyright © 2013 by James E. Nipp
All rights reserved.

ISBN-13: 9781482032772

ISBN-10: 1482032775

FAITH
Journeys

Stories To Inspire Your Faith

Authored by: **JAMES E. NIPP**

Edited by: **KAREN ROBERTS**

This book is dedicated to my wife, Mary, my daughters, Sally, Sara, and Rachel, and my grandchildren and great-grandchildren. Also to the many wonderful people in multicultural international settings who have influenced my life, shared their faith, and helped in shaping and molding me in my faith journey.

Contents

Foreword by Curtis Ferrell	xiii
Preface	xv
Acknowledgements	xix
Part I	1
Early Years of Faith and African Adventures	*1*
1 Captain of the Ship	3
2 Prayers of a Loving Father	9
3 Spiritual Awakening	11
4 Rabid Dog	15
5 The Lame Walks Again	19
6 Our Daughter Lives Again	25
7 The Little Dirt Road	31
8 The Book in the Boat	37
9 The Road South to the Kgotla	41
10 The Blind Man	51
11 The Sick Woman	55

12	Powdered Milk	57
13	The Village Reader	61
14	Math Miracle	65

Part II — 71

African Snake Encounters and God's Protecting Hand — 71

15	The Cobra in the Field	73
16	Cobra Capture	75
17	Double Danger	79
18	Almost Blinded	83
19	Black Mamba	87
20	A Cobra Comes to Church	91
21	The Cobra and the Mother Hen	95
22	The Black Mamba in the Living Room	97

Part III — 101

The Caribbean, Latin America, and Later Years — 101

23	Village Lanterns	103
24	The Rental	107
25	Kindness of a Haitian Grandmother	111
26	A Child's Love for His Papa	115
27	She Gave out of Her Poverty	121
28	The Man under the Bridge	125

Contents

29	Marvin	131
30	The Windblown Bible	135
31	The Flat Tire	137
32	Haggai Experience	139

Photo Gallery	143
Author Biography	147
World Missionary Association	149

Foreword

When I moved to New Castle, Indiana, fifteen years ago with my wife and two young daughters, little did we know that we were moving to the epicenter of corn, soybeans, and basketball … not necessarily in that order. Since then we've learned the difference between seed corn, field corn, and sweet corn. We've also learned about no-till soybeans and class basketball. We've taken seasonal residence in the world's "largest and finest high school basketball field house" and visited the gym where the movie "Hoosiers" was filmed. We also met Jim and Mary Nipp, two of the most famous people in the world—at least to the citizens of Botswana.

Out of this beautiful, small, central Indiana town, one that seems to have jumped off of the canvas of a Norman Rockwell painting, came two young people who believed that God was calling them to something bigger. They were taking God's great good news to Africa! Before Jim and Mary booked passage across the Atlantic in the belly of an ocean freighter, they had already seen the miraculous hand of God at work in their lives. By the time Jim was a teenager he had already been rescued from death multiple times. Each one of these crises, when met with faith, became foundation blocks that would be needed to help Jim and Mary stand firm in the years to come. Foundation blocks that eventually would establish a church in Botswana, one that in turn would train that country's spiritual and civil leaders of today.

These short anecdotes from their lives take you on the wonderful rollercoaster of serving God. From rabid dogs to torrential downpours on dangerous mountain roads; from a small book found in the bottom of a boat to menacing nocturnal visitors on a plain in Central Africa; from one continent to another, and still another, God continually revealed his faithfulness. As you read this compilation of adventures and see the hand of God at work in the lives of Jim and Mary, you may even begin to see the hand of God at work in your life as well! And if that happens, all of the time and effort put into this book will be well worth it.

Faith Journeys

For, you see, if God can take two young people from a small town in central Indiana and transform a nation, what could he do in your life? What would happen if God was allowed to shape and form your life like he did with Jim and Mary? What if God is calling you to something bigger? Your life may never be glamorous, but I will guarantee you it will never be boring, as you can clearly see in the following pages. Enjoy the adventure, and then write the next chapter!

Curt Ferrell
Author, songwriter, and scout for God's new country

Preface

*"I have been crucified with Christ and I no longer live,
but Christ lives in me. The life I now live in the body,
I live by faith in the Son of God, who loved me
and gave himself for me."* **Galatians 2:20**

*"We are the clay, you are the potter; we are all
the work of your hand."* **Isaiah 64:8**

Faith Journeys is a collection of true stories from experiences my wife and I had as missionaries. Join us on the journey of faith, going along the paths with us into the unknown. Read about trusting God in the face of danger, and see how God-ordered intersections with people and situations lead to divine interventions. Each story provides a spiritual insight into everyday issues of life. At the end of your journey with us, you will find your faith strengthened, encouragement to meet your next difficult situation, and new understanding about how God works in our lives to achieve his purposes.

Part I: Early Years of Faith and African Adventures

Part I of our faith journey begins in the Midwest in a small, eastern Indiana town and ends up in Botswana, deep in the remote parts of Africa in the Okavango Delta. Each story reveals how our faith interacts with the faith of others to bring resolution to difficult situations. The school song "Anywhere O Lord with Thee" from my alma mater, Mid-America

Christian University, includes the words, *"Anywhere thy steps we'll follow, on a desert though it be."* Little did I realize when the song was sung that those steps would lead Mary and me into Africa's Kalahari Desert. As you journey with us in these life-changing events, your faith will be strengthened when facing your difficult situations.

Part II: African Snake Encounters and God's Protecting Hand

Part II continues our African stories, these centering on unexpected encounters with deadly poisonous snakes. Around the world, poisonous snakes bite over 40,000 people each year. Botswana has its share of the top ten most deadly snakes of the world. Our encounters with some of the most dangerous snakes on the African continent reveal the continual hand of protection of God in the face of danger, and how faith in God brought resolution to situations that could have been disastrous. As you read these accounts, you will find encouragement and strengthened faith to meet the unknowns in your life.

Part III: The Caribbean, Latin America, and Later Years

Part III begins in the Caribbean and Latin America and ends up back in the Midwest in the USA. These stories center on events and interactions with people that lead to divine interventions. As you read the stories, you will be able to obtain greater understanding about the plan of God and how he works to achieve his purpose. You will find how divine messages from God occur in response to faith, and how God continues to respond by providing resolution to situations in your journey of faith.

As you prepare to read, let me give you a little background about Mary and me, how our faith enabled us to share the love of God with others around the world, and how the faith of others strengthened us. It will shed some light on how we respond as we do to the challenges of our faith journey.

The beginning of my faith journey was growing up in a Christian home in a small town in eastern Indiana. My parents were faithful believers in Christ. My father, a firefighter, was deeply devoted to God and was always helping others. As a child, I saw my father clean and repair broken used toys that had been collected to give to needy children. At

xvi

Preface

Christmastime, I would go with my parents to deliver gifts and toys to families in need. My mother was active in children's vacation Bible schools and was an advocate in assisting battered women.

Other members of my family influenced my early years as well. My aunt Kathryn gave her life as a missionary in India. She, too, was a strong influence in my life. My aunt Betty and uncle David were pastors in Virginia. My uncle Cyrus went to China with an agricultural ministry team. Other members of my family were also involved in Christian ministries.

I was one of three children born to my mom and dad in the 1930s. Our family lived in a modest, low-middle income home. We were members of the Church of God. As a young teenager, I taught the Sunday school class for young boys. These influences played a part in the foundation of my spiritual development.

Mary grew up in the same town and attended the same high school. She had six sisters and seven brothers. Her father was a factory worker and received a limited income. Her mother was a faithful Christian. At thirteen years old, Mary taught a young girl's Sunday school class at church. She was an honor student in high school and sang in the school choir.

Mary and I met at a revival service at the Nazarene church where she attended. We were married in our hometown. We said good-bye to our families and our little Indiana town when we left for Africa to serve as missionaries in 1962. Our three daughters were born outside the USA during our years of living and working overseas as missionaries.

Married over fifty years, Mary and I have traveled and lived in several different multicultural environments around the world. Now as great-grandparents, we look back on a lifetime of memories and reflect on the many ways our lives have been spiritually shaped and molded. We have been blessed as a result of our interaction with others. We have witnessed faith in action in the lives of many people. We have seen events unfold in our lives that defy explanation and can only be described as miracles. We have witnessed the protecting hand of God in death-defying circumstances.

I feel a compelling need to share our story with others, being reminded of what Jesus said in Luke 18:8: *"When the Son of Man comes, will he find faith on the earth?"* May your faith be strengthened and you be inspired and challenged as you read about our journey of faith.

Acknowledgments

I want to thank the many people who have inspired my faith and encouraged me as I reached out over the years to point others to Christ.

I deeply appreciate my wife, Mary, who has faithfully stood by my side in our faith journey, always there to encourage me in the difficult times. I thank our three daughters, Sally, Sara, and Rachel, who sacrificed with us in our years of serving others.

I thank the many individuals who inspired my faith and taught me lessons on how to better understand the reality of life from their perspective. These include, but are not limited to, the man under the bridge, the village reader, the Haitian grandmother and the young man with Muscular Dystrophy.

I thank those who challenged me to share our faith journey by encouraging us to put our stories in book form—more individuals than I can list.

I thank author Donna Thomas, pastor Bob Lines, and teacher Ivan Rosalia for their endorsement of the book.

I thank pastor Curtis Ferrell for his backing and support of producing this book.

I thank Karen Roberts of RQuest for editing the book and preparing it for publication.

Above all, I thank God for allowing us the opportunity to share our faith journey.

Part I

*Early Years of Faith
and African Adventures*

1

Captain of the Ship

"Or take ships as an example. Although they are so large and are driven by strong winds, they are steered by a very small rudder wherever the pilot wants to go." **James 3:4**

It was midnight, with a full moon, when the sound of the ship's horn signaled we were on our way. As my wife and I sailed out of New York Harbor in May 1962 aboard the African Gulf, a small ocean freighter, a foamy wake trailed behind. Mary and I fixed our eyes on the harbor as we glided quietly past the Statue of Liberty. Soon the skyline of New York City faded over the horizon, and we found ourselves in the darkness of the Atlantic Ocean.

With a crew of thirty-five men including the ship's officers, there was space for only eight additional passengers. Mary and I had purchased one-way tickets to Dar es Salaam, Tanganyika, now called Tanzania, and were on our way to serve as missionaries. Another missionary couple was also on board the cargo ship, which was destined to deliver goods to the coastal cities in southeast Africa. A Wisconsin dairy farmer and a Chicago owner of a restaurant chain were going to Africa on a hunting expedition, and their four-wheel-drive vehicle was on board the freighter as well. The other two passengers were South African citizens returning home after a visit in the USA.

Faith Journeys

Our first night at sea was one of excitement and apprehension as we adjusted to the adventure of ocean sailing. It was a restless night in the cabin on the rolling sea. We had been instructed to use the safety straps on our bunks to ensure we would be secure from falling in case the ship should suddenly pitch. The droning sound of the engine created a noise to which we would become accustomed in the ensuing days of our journey.

It would be nearly a month at sea before we would arrive at Dar es Salam, located on the east coast of Africa. The ship would be sailing around the southern tip of Africa, stopping at several ports to unload and load freight, before Mary and I would arrive at our final destination. As passengers we were to have our meals in the officer's dining room, giving us opportunity to become acquainted with the captain, other officers of the ship, and each other. Over the course of our long journey, mealtimes became our social time, and we all became good friends. Since there was little else to do on board, we looked forward to those hours when we could chat and joke with one another in the dining hall.

Because our journey across the sea would be long, Mary and I and the other missionary couple on board asked the captain of the ship for permission to have church services on the ship's deck each Sunday morning. He agreed. Attendees at the services included other passengers, the crew, and ship officers, including the captain.

In time it became easier to sleep all night and rest peacefully. The drone of the engine was always present, and the fresh, salty sea air and sound of the waves created a pleasant environment. Our cabins were small, with a porthole view out onto the deck. Our sleeping arrangements were built-in bunks along the wall. While comfortable, we were still on a freighter. It was certainly not passenger ship luxury.

Early one morning, I was awakened by unexpected silence. The sun had just broken over the horizon, and it shined through the porthole onto the floor in the cabin. The stillness was startling because we had become so accustomed to the engine's sounds. I felt for the safety strap on my bed that I had secured for the night. It was stretched tight against my side. I had rolled tightly against the strap because the ship had listed to one side. In the eerie quietness, I could no longer hear the engine.

As I unfastened my strap, I nearly fell out of bed. I dressed quickly, having to adjust my balance because the floor of the cabin was slanted. Moving carefully to maintain my balance, I walked out of the cabin and made my way across the deck towards the steps leading to the next level.

I climbed the steps to the ship's control room. There I saw the captain at the wheel and other officers busy working.

As politely as I could, I asked the captain what was happening. In response, he explained calmly that there had been a major breakdown in the engine. The engine had to be shut down. Without power, all forward motion had ceased. During the night, the ship had slowed to a stop, causing it to list to one side. At present we were adrift.

The captain continued, explaining that the crew was pumping fuel from one side to the other in an effort to balance the ship. He went on to say he was not sure when the ship could be repaired. A vehicle breakdown on a highway was one thing, but to have an engine fail on an ocean freighter in the mid-Atlantic was quite different. It was then that I learned the ship was a very old freighter and was, in fact, making its last trip before it was scrapped. That explained the special fare we were given for our one-way tickets.

Adrift at sea was not exactly in our plans. We had no way to send personal messages to anyone, and people were scheduled to meet Mary and me in Tanzania on June 20. What would they do if they arrived and found no ship in the harbor? We had no idea how long we would be drifting at sea and even if the ship could be repaired.

It was a weird feeling as my wife and I sat silently on the deck that day, adrift in the middle of the ocean. Only the sound of waves slapping at the sides of the ship could be heard. The foamy wake of the ship we'd grown accustomed to had disappeared, and we drifted throughout the day and into the night.

A general concern and anxiety swept across the other passengers as well. Our ship, alone, in the middle of the Atlantic, was bobbing on the waves like a cork. The more experienced ocean travelers seemed to take the crisis in stride, but this was Mary and my's first ocean voyage. Extra anxiety had just been added to our lives.

I was facing a new test in my journey of faith. I could not see beyond the horizon. Not knowing what would happen next challenged my faith in a way I had not yet experienced. I had faced crises in my life before and had managed to survive, so I understood how I must place my faith and trust in Christ. I believed that Jesus was the Captain of my life. I often referenced Proverbs 3:5–6, *"Trust in the Lord with all your heart and lean not on your own understanding; in all your ways submit to him, and he will make your paths straight."* There was more for me yet to discover about faith. This ocean journey had put me once again on the potter's wheel so that I would be shaped and molded for the Master's use.

After being adrift three days at sea, all sense of direction was gone. With the sun overhead at high noon and no reference points, I was clueless where north and south or east and west were. I assumed our ship was still on course for Cape Town, South Africa, our first port of call. After all, when we left New York City, we were headed in that direction. The rising and setting of the sun was our only measure of the passing of time.

The anxiety of the situation washed ashore at us in waves of concern, creating doubt and eroding trust. Our minds focused on when or even if the ship would be repaired and when we could be on our way again. Not only had I lost my sense of physical direction, but spiritually I was allowing doubt and fear to eat away at my faith. My faith was awash in a sea of doubt, and I did not know what was ahead.

In the midst of my personal crisis, I suddenly heard excited voices. It was the crew. Puffs of black smoke began to billow from the ship's stack, and the sound of the engine starting up filled the air. The ship slowly began to move. We were on our way once again. I felt a tremendous sense of ease and relief. All my anxiety had been in vain. My worries were now behind me.

We still had the long journey ahead of us, sailing southeast between South America and the African continent. It was still going to be a long time before we would see land. But my reevaluation of the situation brought a sense of assurance that everything was going to get back to normal. God's Word says, *"Faith is confidence in what we hope for and assurance about what we do not see"* (Hebrews 11:1). My faith at the moment, however, had not been operating by this definition. I had based my positive assumptions on my physical senses, what I could see. Real faith, Scripture said, involves patience and long-suffering as well, based on what we *cannot* yet see.

In my sea journey, I had spent a lot of time on the upper deck where I could see for miles. I loved the ocean breeze, and the sea air was refreshing. From this position, I could see the entire ship from bow to stern. Looking out at the rear of the ship, I could see the foamy wake left by the ship's propellers. It was good to be moving once again.

The sun made visibility of the ship's wake very clear. Normally the wake was a long straight line, but as I watched it, I saw a great arc appearing. In fact, the ship was making a 180 degree turn.

Captain of the Ship

As I watched this view unfolding before my eyes, a new rush of anxiety raced through me, triggering my impulsive nature to respond. My humanity sent my mind into a whirlwind of assumptions. What I could not understand was that in my journey of faith on the sea, a loving God was preparing me for yet another test, one of many more trials ahead in which I would have to place my trust totally in Christ alone.

God knew this little Indiana boy had a lot to learn. Back home in church services, I would not hesitate to raise my hand and sing, "I'll go where you want me to go, dear Lord." But like the disciples, who fearfully went into panic on the stormy sea after Jesus had clearly said, *"Let us go to the other side."* (Mark 4:35) so was I. My immediate assumption, after the ship began to move again, was that we were heading in the direction of Cape Town; so this arc, I assumed, indicated we were turning back to New York.

My ease of mind when the ship started moving again had been short-lived. Questions and assumptions began flooding my mind. Had the crew repaired the ship just enough to take it back to the harbor in New York? In my fear, I was convinced of this. In my journey of faith, since I could not see over my horizon, I again was allowing my anxiety to dictate my actions instead of "leaning on the everlasting arms," as I had often sung. I had lost my sense of direction again and did not realize it.

It was clear to me we had turned around. How could I resolve this problem? What about those who were scheduled to meet Mary and me? How could we get word to them? All kinds of questions and fears entered my mind. I began to try to calculate what we were going to do. We had limited funds and no family in New York City. Where were we going to stay in New York on our return?

Anxiety and frustration built as I found myself running to the captain. I raced across the deck and up the steps to the control room. As I entered, I am sure the stately, older captain could see the anxiety in my troubled, young face. "What is happening?" I asked. "Why are we going back? The ship has turned 180 degrees."

The captain smiled and looked directly at me. "Yes, we have turned 180 degrees. We did turn around, but we are not going back to New York City." He patiently went on to explain. "You see, for three days we sat motionless, no power to move. We drifted off course, listing to one side, causing the ship to completely turn around. Once we had the power to move again, I corrected our drifting error and set us back on course. We are now back on course for our destination."

The captain's words put my mind at ease. I realized this event was a learning experience for me. The captain was in control of all the events involving the ship. He knew how to solve the problems and put the ship back on course. In a rush of insight, I understood that our Captain, Jesus, is fully aware of our drifting, lack of power, and inability to move forward for him when things go wrong. Only he can set us back on course. That night I was able to rest peacefully, knowing that the Captain was in control.

I have never forgotten my experience at sea. It has impacted my life, enabling me to weather many storms and stay on course. My faith and reliance on God, who alone is the God of all circumstances, was strengthened for the long journey ahead.

"We must pay the most careful attention, therefore, to what we have heard, so that we do not drift away." **(Hebrews 2:1)**

2

Prayers of a Loving Father

"Then I will give him to the LORD for all the days of his life." **1 Samuel 1:11**

I was born at home in the 1930s on Vine Street in New Castle, Indiana. It was a quiet, little, eastern Indiana town. In those days, it was common practice for birth to take place at home. Newborn care did not include hospitalization, incubators, or specialized trauma care as today. There were no fetal monitors or other means to ensure a safe delivery or stability for newborns, and doctors with their little black bags still made house calls.

Just before the time of my birth, the doctor was notified and arrived at the house for the delivery. It soon became apparent that complications were developing. While not uncommon, the umbilical cord was wrapped around my neck, and I had been deprived of oxygen to the point that I had turned blue as a result of compression of the umbilical cord and heart issues.

The doctor did the best he could to stabilize me, but he gave little hope of survival. He told my father that I would most likely die within twenty-four hours. Being born as what was termed a "blue baby" almost always resulted in death in those days. He left the house as my parents did what they could to keep me comfortable.

My father, a devout Christian, pleaded with God in faith to allow me to live. I was his firstborn son, and he made a vow with God that if I would be spared, he would give me to the service of the Lord. He understood that such a commitment would have to be a personal choice by me.

God spared my life that cold winter day in 1939. At an early age, I didn't know of my father's prayer the night of my birth, but it was clear to me that I was called to multicultural ministry.

Many years later, when I was back in the USA after several years on the mission field, my father went to be with the Lord. I was in my forties at the time. One day while talking with my mother, she told me about the prayer of my father the night I was born. She explained how God had honored my father's faith and performed a miracle for him to witness. God had called me to missionary ministry, she said, and I had responded to that call, unaware of my father's prayer.

I have walked through "the valley of the shadow of death." numerous times since my birth. Through faith and obedience to God, I have survived extremely dangerous circumstances. Each time my faith has been strengthened. I am a servant of Christ, a soul on assignment, placed in a physical body. I am here to share my story now because of a miracle at birth as a result of the prayers of a loving father and the continuing hand of a protecting God.

3

Spiritual Awakening

"God spoke to him in this way." **Acts 7:6**

The voice of God can be and often is recognized at an early age. With it also comes the opportunity to choose. That choice, and the many that come after it, impacts our eternal destiny.

I was five years old when I first heard the voice of God. It was the "gentle whisper" of God the prophet Elijah experienced (1 Kings 19:12) that first stimulated my spiritual awareness. Perhaps it is a simple story, but I find it exciting how the gentle voice of God has been speaking to mankind, one person at a time, for endless generations.

How we respond to the call of God is relative to our cultural environment and the influences on our lives. When encountering disastrous events, personal tragedies, accidents, or health issues, most people's first response is to call out to God. That response can be with anger, or it may be in faith, believing God is in control. Even in the most adverse conditions in life, many individuals still choose to respond in faith to the voice of God. God is able to shape and mold our lives regardless of circumstances that may surround us.

Psychologists might say my mind at this young age was being programmed by parental influence, for we all are products of our environment. It is true to a certain extent; however, I believe there is more to it than simple psychological conditioning. I believe the Spirit of God speaks directly to all souls. I believe people of all ages and cultures can hear the inner voice of God reaching into their souls. God is waiting for every human who is yearning for help. We have the choice to listen or to ignore God's voice.

My journey of faith began in the small town of New Castle, Indiana, in 1944. A small "mom and pop" grocery store was located near my home, and when my mother would go to the store, she would often take me along. The store had a row of glass containers filled with cookies in front of the checkout counter. Each cookie jar had a glass lid. Packaging of cookies was not a common practice in those days. Customers would open the lids and take out the cookies they wanted to purchase, and the grocer would place them in a bag. As a five-year-old boy, those containers were easily within my reach.

My parents had taught me some things about right and wrong, but the concept of stealing had not fully registered in my mind at this point. I assumed all cookies in life were free. In times past, I would open one of those lids, take out a cookie, and eat it. What I did not know was my mother would always pay the grocer for the cookie.

One day while at the store with my mother, I wanted a cookie. But this time it was different. Somehow, in my mind, I realized those cookies were not really mine and free, and that to take a cookie without permission or arrangements to pay would be wrong. My desire for a cookie, however, was not diminished by this insight.

I found myself at a point of decision. A spiritual awakening was taking place, and I found myself having to make a choice. Would I yield to the temptation, or would I take the proper action and ask? I certainly did not have the money to pay for the cookie, and I certainly did not want to hear my mom say no. And so I yielded to the temptation.

The memory is still crystal clear in my mind. I recall looking at the grocer and my mom. I recall how I watched the grocer and my mom talking. When I knew they were not looking, I quietly lifted the lid from the cookie jar. In the past I would take a cookie and just start eating it. This time was different. I carefully hid the cookie in my pocket, keeping a close eye on my mom and the grocer.

Spiritual Awakening

As my mom and I left the store, I felt terrible. My head hung down as I walked alongside her. I had tears in my eyes. I was walking guilt. At home, when my mom wasn't looking, I ate the cookie. It tasted terrible. So strong was my guilt that I cleared the crumbs from my pocket so mom would not find them when she did the laundry.

I was hiding in my "garden of Eden," and God was asking me, "Where are you?" as he did Adam (Genesis 3:9). God knew where I was; God cared, God loved me, and he was patiently trying to mold and shape me into the person I needed to be. For the next years, I harbored that experience deep in my heart. Even as the experience was suppressed, it would surface from time to time.

When I was nine years old, my church held a revival. Back then a revival was a week of special services, one every evening. My family always attended every service. I developed a deep interest in the services and listened intensely as the minister preached. At the end of the service one evening, the God who was there when I took the cookie let me know he was there with me and was still patiently waiting for me. I felt a gentle tugging in my heart. My Creator, the God who gave me life, still loved me. He knew how I was struggling and trying to make my way through life on my own. He knew I needed guidance in making choices. The memory of the cookie returned and replayed in my mind.

The gentle whisper of the spirit of God came to me once again, reminding me of what my proper behavior should be. As the congregation was singing softly, tears came to my eyes, and I spontaneously went to the altar of the church to pray. Through repentance, I found redemption, freedom from guilt, and a new beginning.

That evening I felt it a miracle that I, one in billions of souls over the generations, would still be so loved that I would be spoken to directly by my Creator. The Spirit of God had placed my soul, like clay, on the proverbial potter's wheel to shape and mold it.

God's great love encompasses all his creation, yet he sees each of us as individuals. He reaches out to us one by one. I firmly believe that a continual miracle takes place when God, the Creator of all, speaks gently to us. He wants to guide and direct our paths. He desires to shape and mold us into the people we should be. How we respond to God's gentle voice determines our eternal destiny.

4

Rabid Dog

"Obey the LORD by doing what I tell you. Then it will go well with you, and your life will be spared." **Jeremiah 38:20**

It was the end of a typical school day in Indiana. I was in the fourth grade, and my sister Rebekah was in the sixth. She and I always walked to and from school, just as many children did in those days. School was only about a half mile from our home. Being an average kid, I would skip along on my way, often checking the railroad ditch for crawfish. I felt secure in my tranquil world.

At the sound of the dismissal bell at the end of school that day, we gathered our books and started for home. Rebekah was walking about a half a block ahead of me. I was skipping along to catch up with her when the unexpected happened.

We had walked that route many times before without any problems, but on that afternoon, a dog came running toward me. It jumped up, grabbed me by my right arm, and sunk its teeth in deep. Terrified, I cried out to my sister, who turned to see what had happened. Rebekah came running back to me. She examined my arm that was bleeding. And as a big sister would do, she comforted me as we continued on home.

When we arrived home and entered the house, I was still emotionally distraught over the attack by the dog. My mom realized there was a crisis when she saw my torn coat and tears. While my sister explained what had happened, Mom cleaned my wound and bandaged it. She then called my dad, who was working, to let him know.

Dad came home to check on me and learn more about what had taken place. He was always there for me when I needed him. I told him how the dog just suddenly jumped from the grassy bank in the yard and grabbed me by the arm. I explained I did not know if it was going to continue attacking, so I got away from it as soon as possible. After examining my arm, he gave me a hug of assurance that everything would be okay.

Rabies was not an issue in our area at the time. Pets were not even required to have rabies shots in those days. The disease was not high on the list of concerns for the general population, so nobody thought too much about the possibility of there being rabies among the area animals. As a precaution, however, my father contacted the police about the incident. The police told him another child had been bitten recently as well, and they said they would talk to the dog's owner and advise him to secure the dog and keep an eye on it.

A few weeks went by, and the wound on my arm healed. We had heard nothing about the status of the dog until a police car pulled up at our house late at night. The officer came to the door and talked to my parents. I was not sure what was happening, but after he left, they were very disturbed. The police had informed them that the dog that had bitten me had died. Not only had it died, but also the owners, fearing the consequence, had buried the dog, not telling anyone. Someone who knew about the matter had contacted the police. The police then ordered the dog owners to retrieve the dog, and it was sent off for testing. It would be several days, they said, before the results could be obtained.

This news was an unexpected shock to my parents, and it was emotionally disturbing. My mom was in tears, and I could see anxiety and fear on my father's face. I was rushed off to the hospital that night, where as a precaution, the doctors began rabies shots. They said the incubation time for me had reached a critical margin. My parents contacted people everywhere to begin praying.

In the 1940s, a series of twenty-three rabies shots was required. I was about a week into the shots when my parents were informed that the tests on the dog showed it was rabid. By this time, the rabies shots were having adverse effects on me. My arms were swollen and burned like fire. My abdomen was extremely painful and inflamed. As a result, the doctor had to find new areas on my body to inject the shots, which were administered every morning and afternoon.

People everywhere were praying. A rabies quarantine was declared by county officials. Other rabid animals were found in the area. My condition seemed to be deteriorating, and my folks were devastated but continued praying. I saw their concern, and also saw their faith as well as the faith of others who were praying.

At the end of the series of twenty-three rabies shots, I was extremely ill and in terrible pain. My arms and legs were swollen and inflamed. It was months before I could overcome the complications.

The inoculations and reactions took a toll on me emotionally as well. I was in a dreamy daze. I felt at peace with God, yet I did not fully understand the complexity of the situation. I just knew I felt terrible and was in continual pain. I trusted, however, in the faith I saw witnessed in the lives of my parents and many church friends. I knew it was through the power and mercy of God that my life had been spared.

A stone in the foundation of faith God was building in my life had been added. I had overcome a frightful experience, and through the faith of those who surrounded my family in prayer and the faith I saw in my parents, I realized how great God was to spare me. My faith was beginning to grow.

This event was just the beginning of many that would happen to me as a result of the encounter with the rabid dog. Each event would play a part in shaping and molding my faith and understanding of how God orchestrates the outcome of circumstances in life. He was shaping and molding me like a potter does to clay. Each event was another stone to the foundation of my faith.

5

The Lame Walks Again

"'He himself bore our sins' in his body on the cross, so that we might die to sins and live for righteousness; 'by his wounds you have been healed.'" **1 Peter 2:24**

From the time of the episode with the rabid dog, my health seemed destined to one crisis after another. I survived severe pneumonia and more than one measles episode with accompanying high fevers. Still, I was an upbeat kid. I had determined that my calling in life was to be one of service to others, and nothing could stop me.

By age ten, I felt an urgency to take the good news of Christ to all who would listen. I envisioned a life of service in multicultural, international ministry. My mother's sister was serving as a missionary in India. An uncle had served in China in a Christian agricultural ministry. Others of my family were in ministry as well. I liked to envision myself somewhere overseas. What I didn't understand at the time was that God's plan for my life would require many more faith-building events.

Complications from the series of rabies shots had taken its toll on my immune system, resulting in my not fully regaining good health. At twelve years old, I became very ill again. My aunt Ethel had died recently of tuberculosis, and I had been exposed to the disease through visits with her. I had to be tested, and the skin test results came back positive. After additional tests and X-rays, doctors reported they had found dark areas in my lungs.

I was running a continual fever. I suffered extensive joint pain and loss of energy. Further testing confirmed I also had developed Rheumatic fever. Then the doctors found a heart murmur. They did the best they could to treat my many ailments, but the health care system in the 1950s was limited in comparison to today's technological advances.

My overall health condition rapidly deteriorated. I was no longer able to attend classes at school, so I did all my studies at home. Fellow students would bring my assignments to my home, and the teacher would visit and tutor me when possible. I had become very weak, so I spent most of my days in bed or in a recliner chair. My ability to walk was diminishing.

In this weakened state, my immune system began to fail. My kidneys were being affected. I was diagnosed with nephritis, a disease affecting the kidneys that in those days was generally fatal. As in the rabid dog event, my parents were devastated; however, they had a strong faith in God and believed that somehow the issues would be resolved.

I was in and out of the hospital for several months without seeing any improvement. The doctors finally told my parents there was little more they could do. They said it would take a miracle for me to survive.

I remained upbeat. Our local church would prepare what they called "sunshine boxes" and bring them by. The decorated boxes, made by the people of the church, would contain small, wrapped gifts. My mother would permit me to open one gift each day. It became the highlight of each day. My father helped me build a crystal radio, and he installed an antenna outside my bedroom window. I would spend hours listening to foreign radio stations as well as local Christian stations.

People would often stop by to visit to cheer me up. Whenever someone asked me what I wanted to do when I grew up, my reply would never waver. "I am going to the mission field and preach the gospel." I would see tears in my father's eyes. He well remembered my difficult life to this point, and he remembered his promise to God when I was born. He had prayed that if God would spare my life, he would give me over to his service.

The local doctors had given up hope on my recovery. They had exhausted all their knowledge regarding what to do in my complicated case. I still recall the day I overheard the doctor talking with my parents in the next room. He told them he would arrange for me to be moved to a children's hospital fifty miles away in Indianapolis. It was considered the only possible hope of my survival. My parents notified all the area churches and Christians they knew everywhere to continue special prayer in my behalf.

In the meantime, I had been writing letters to people at Christian radio stations I listened to on the crystal radio my dad had helped me build. I wrote about my plans to go to the mission field. People at the radio station established communication with my parents, and my parents requested the radio audience to pray for my healing.

As I look back on my health crises, I still recall the positive feelings I had that everything was going to be okay. My faith had been tested before, and I believed somehow God would bring resolution to my crises. My faith was strong and my vision focused. I was convinced I would someday serve as a missionary on a foreign field.

The doctor had arranged for one more series of tests at the local hospital before transferring me to the children's hospital in Indianapolis. On the morning of those tests, my father came to my bedroom to get me. He carried me to the car because I was too weak to walk on my own. At the hospital, he carried me in. I was given the scheduled tests, and then my mother and dad and I sat together in the examination room, waiting for the doctor to return with his report.

As I sat there on an examination table with my legs dangling over the side, I began to feel a tingling sensation moving over my body. It was almost like an electric current. I felt strength coming over me. My legs began to swing. I was feeling great.

The doctor walked in the room and looked at me, unaware of what had taken place in my body. He looked over his test results and then back at me again. There was a puzzled look on his face. He had been monitoring my illness for several months, and knew my condition. He explained that there was something strange with the outcome of the tests. "We need to take some more tests," he said. "Our results may be wrong."

When he asked me how I was feeling, I smiled and said, "Great." He asked me if I felt I could stand on my own. "I believe so," I said, and then I stood up. He was amazed.

The doctor ordered more tests, and when he came back in the room the next time, he excitedly told my folks the news. All tests results had come back perfect. Kidneys, lungs, blood, X-rays—everything showed perfect health. The heart murmur had disappeared as well. Not only were the tests perfect, he said, but they showed no trace I had ever been ill! He told my folks that the only explanation was an absolute miracle from God.

As we left the doctor that day, I skipped to the car, smiling. Tears flowed down my parents' faces. In the car, I asked my dad to take me to my grandparents' house. I wanted to tell them. On arrival I jumped out of the car, ran in the front door, and bounded through the house, yelling, "I am healed!" I exited the back door of the house and ran across the yard toward my cousin's house. I jumped clear of the fence by his house. I shared the good news with him as well.

After my dramatic healing, I returned to school and remained focused on my plans to prepare myself for a ministry among the poor in other lands. In time I found myself working at the Christian radio station that I had discovered with the headphones and crystal radio my dad and I had made several years before.

God honored the faith of many that day. I firmly believe the timing of the healing was orchestrated by God. I kept my Bible on my bed stand and faithfully read from it every day. I would read every book I could get my hands on about missions. The events in my life helped me understand the pain and suffering of others. The crises in my life gave strength to my faith in God. Each experience was another stone in the foundation that God was laying for my life. I was like clay in the hands of a potter, being prepared to go through the fire.

I believe that God, our Creator, has the power and ability to alter physical events at any time. Physical healing is not the only miracle that God is capable of performing, however. God can heal broken hearts. He can heal broken relationships. God will be with us in our pain and suffering, and he will walk by our side or carry us in our difficult times. While God has the power to perform unexplainable miracles, the transformation of the soul and preparation for eternal life is the greatest of miracles.

I am always cautious to point out that healing or resolving a health crisis may take many forms. Our humanity focuses on the physical. We all would like to remain young and healthy forever. But in reality, we are souls in a loaned, physical body. We are here only for a short time.

Faith includes acceptance of the outcome of all situations. We will all experience our final heartbeat and take our last breath. Life is a gift, and from time to time, God extends our time as he wills.

6

Our Daughter Lives Again

"My daughter has just died. But come and put your hand on her, and she will live." **Matthew 9:18**

Mary was a senior in high school when we met at a revival at church in our hometown in 1958. I was home for a visit from college in Houston, Texas. Mary was going to be attending Ball State University in Muncie, Indiana. For the next few years, we kept in touch by mail and got to see each other during breaks from school. We were married in 1961.

Mary and I both had felt the call to missions during our childhood, and God had confirmed it again and again. In January of 1962, we drove from Indiana to Alberta, Canada, to meet with the people of a small missionary board that was going to assist us in obtaining legal permits to work in Africa for a year. I was ordained as a minister in Alberta, Canada, while there.

We began working to pay off our debts in preparation to go to Africa to serve as missionaries. Meanwhile, we were traveling and visiting congregations, sharing our vision. We also were studying Swahili to enable us to be prepared to communicate with the people with whom we were going to be working. A lot of preparation was going on to make this first assignment of our calling to serve God as missionaries a reality.

When the time of our departure to Africa arrived at last, we were ready and excited to be on our way. We loaded our steamer trunks and few belongings into a travel trailer. Mary's brother drove us to New York City so we could sail from there to Africa. The night before we sailed, Mary became ill with motion sickness when we rode the Staten Island Ferry over to Jersey City. She was expecting our first child, so we knew this trip was to be a difficult and long journey for her. She certainly was making a tremendous sacrifice to travel over a month at sea in her condition.

After arriving in Tanzania, we traveled to the mountainous area of Kainam, high above the town of Mbula. The little "tin can" house provided for us was a simple wood frame structure wrapped in corrugated metal with a metal roof. Built on a concrete slab, it had just two small rooms. The bedroom had space for a bed with limited walk-around space. The other room of the house, the kitchen, had a small table and a crude stand with a wash pan. We stacked our steamer trunks and used wood crates to serve as furniture. A kerosene lantern lit our home at night. Our outdoor toilet was shared by the people of the church. With our few material belongings, we had enough to survive.

Our little place was beautiful to us. It was located high above the cloud level of the African Rift Valley below. We could see both Mt. Kilimanjaro and Mt. Meru, an ancient volcano, from our mountain home.

Our daughter, Sally was born at the Mt. Meru hospital in Arusha, Tanzania, located about 150 miles from our little mountain mission home. At three months old, she developed dysentery. We took what we thought were all the necessary precautions to prevent dehydration and resolve the problem.

Medical care at the time was difficult to reach from our location, high in the mountains and accessible only by a narrow, hand-cut dirt road along the side of the mountain. Even in the best of conditions, the road was very dangerous for travel. There were no guardrails on the winding, steep, and treacherous road. During rains, it was all but impassible and subject to landslides. The uncertainty that the handmade road could give way under our vehicle was always on our minds as we traveled it.

The small hospital located nearest to us in the valley below had very limited services. It was not staffed or equipped to address major medical emergencies. Because of our concern for our daughter, we took her to that hospital. Medication was prescribed and provided to correct her dysentery problem. Little did we know at the time that when the medication was mixed, the druggist miscalculated and put a lethal dose of morphine in it.

After that trip to the valley hospital, we returned to our little mission home in the mountains and gave Sally the prescribed medication prepared at the hospital, confident it would give her the help she needed. We gave her as much liquid to drink as possible to prevent dehydration.

That evening, I went to the church for Bible study while Mary remained at the house with our baby. She had worked in nursing prior to our coming to Africa, so we felt comfortable that everything would be fine. In the midst of the Bible study, Mary rushed through the door to tell me our daughter had taken a turn for the worse. I excused myself and rushed to the house, which was next to the church. Our baby was showing signs of oxygen deprivation. Her fingers and toes were turning blue.

We knew we had to take quick, emergency action. We began to pray, calling on God to spare our little girl. I quickly fueled our old Land Rover and prepared to rush our daughter to the nearest hospital that had facilities for emergencies, the hospital where she had been born, 150 miles away in the city of Arusha. The drive down the mountain to the African Rift Valley floor on those narrow, treacherous, switchback dirt roads was frightening, to say the least.

We reached the great north road to Arusha below us without mishap and headed north. We were in a race for time, clinging to our faith, totally unaware that our daughter's vital systems were starting to shut down from an overdose of morphine. She was clinging to life. I drove as fast as I safely could in a race for time. As I drove, we were praying and continually checking our baby. The cyanosis was worsening; she had slipped into a coma and was listless.

Back in the USA, unknown to us at the time, my mother felt an urgent need to pray for her granddaughter. She contacted several others to pray also. This was happening at the same time as we were dealing with the emergency in Africa. She was not aware of our emergency but was overwhelmed with a burden to pray. As prayers were taking place back home, we raced down the north road toward the hospital.

We arrived at the outskirts of the city of Arusha and drove directly to the hospital. Our baby was limp. She had turned blue all over, and her breathing was so shallow it was hard to detect. She was dying in Mary's arms, and there seemed nothing we could do.

At the entrance to Mt. Meru hospital, we jumped out of the vehicle and ran with the baby through the door. It was late at night. We could no longer detect any breathing from our baby. A nurse met us in the hallway of the hospital, and she immediately recognized the emergency we were facing. She grabbed the baby, and we raced into the emergency room. She quickly got a hypodermic needle needed for an injection in an effort to restart her heart.

There were no other workers in the emergency room, so she asked for my help to set up the oxygen system. As she placed a face mask on our baby, I opened the valve on the oxygen tank. Since no doctors were available at the time, the nurse was doing all she could do. She kept checking for a heartbeat with her stethoscope as we administered oxygen and did CPR. Clinically our baby had gone into cardio/respiratory arrest.

Another nurse arrived and quickly left to locate the doctor, who had to come to the hospital from his home. We had the bottle of prescription diarrhea medicine from the other hospital with us, and the nurse took it for analysis, suspecting it could be the problem. After a short time, our daughter showed signs of a weak heartbeat with very shallow breathing.

We were informed that a level of morphine had been detected in the diarrhea medicine that could cause cardio/respiratory arrest in an adult, let alone a child. The morphine overdose in our child had suppressed her systems to the point that she was in a deep coma, and all bodily functions were shutting down. We were still in a very serious crisis.

The doctor and staff were doing all they could to reverse the problem. They continued in their attempt to try to stabilize our baby's heartbeat and breathing. It seemed they were losing the battle. A room was provided for us where we could be alone while they worked with our daughter. Over and over, she went into cardio/respiratory arrest. The hospital staff scrambled, doing all they could to revive her each time. Our hearts were breaking. We wept and called on God to spare our child.

I sent a telegram to family in the USA, requesting urgent prayer for our baby. The telegram just said, PLEASE HAVE URGENT PRAYER FOR SALLY. I did not know they were already in prayer but unaware of what was happening. The Holy Spirit had communicated ahead of our telegram.

God was testing our commitment and our faith and resolve to serve on the mission field. We believed that God was in control of all

Our Daughter Lives Again

circumstances, and we continued to believe that somehow he would bring resolve to our crisis. I send a second telegram home that simply stated, CONTINUE PRAYING.

The hospital staff was not aware that we were missionaries. They just knew we had rushed into the hospital with a dying child. When the doctor came to the room where we were waiting and praying, we could tell by his facial expression that he was not there to give us good news. He began by asking us if we would like for someone to call a priest. He went on to say they had done everything they could possibly do, but the outcome looked grim. Most likely Sally's heart and breathing would shut down again, he said, and chances of reviving her would get slimmer each time. He went on to say that it was likely she already had experienced brain damage.

We were crushed, but our faith in God remained. We knew she was in his hands. We explained to the doctor that a priest would not be necessary; we believed God was in control, and she was in God's hands. We thanked him for all he and the staff were doing and resumed praying. Again and again they struggled to keep her alive, but her heart continued to shut down.

By this time we were exhausted, and it was in the early hours of the morning. In the midst of our grief, weeping, and praying, we were fighting to keep awake. A thousand thoughts raced through our minds. We had given our daughter fully to the hands of God, and we were resolved that God was in control of the situation. We wanted our daughter back, but we were helpless. We knew it would take a miracle, and we needed a miracle.

The hospital had become ghostly quiet. We knew the hospital staff was monitoring our baby while we waited in the nearby room. With our arms around each other, we sat and waited. Every step we heard in the hallway could be someone bringing news about our baby. It did not take the sound of footsteps for us to know God was in control. And then, out of the quietness in the hospital, we heard a faint, weak cry. It was our baby!

We ran into the room. The doctor and nurses indicated that perhaps she might survive, but the doctor called us aside and told us that we should not get our hopes up. He said she could remain in a coma indefinitely and have irreversible brain damage because of what had transpired. But our faith in God gave us peace. If God could give life back to our child, he certainly could restore her from her extended oxygen deprivation.

Our baby was stabilized. She was breathing on her own. Her heartbeat was restored, but she remained in a deep coma. Day and night for a week, we prayed and waited by her side. As Mary sat by Sally's side, she held her hand, prayed, and talked to her. Mary would stay at her side as I went out periodically and brought food back to the hospital for us. The hospital, at its best, did not serve meals.

It was early in the morning after our baby had been in a coma for a week that Mary called to me with excitement. "Jim, she just squeezed my finger! She just squeezed my finger!" I ran to her side, and Sally opened her eyes and looked at us. She did not make a sound, but we knew our Creator, God of the heavens, had given our baby back.

There was a miracle in Arusha that day. Today our daughter is a nurse, both of her children have been on international mission trips, and she is a grandmother and a follower of Christ.

In the apostle Paul's missionary journeys, he continually faced crises. In writing a letter to the Philippians, he advised them, *"Whatever happens, conduct yourselves in a manner worthy of the gospel of Christ."* (Philippians 1:27) We were learning to always place our faith is God in all circumstances.

7

The Little Dirt Road

"Trust in the LORD with all your heart and lean not on your own understanding; in all your ways submit to him, and he will make your paths straight." **Proverbs 3:5–6**

When we were living in Kainam, high in the mountains of Tanzania, we had an old pickup truck with many miles on it. While not the best vehicle, it provided transportation. Sadly, our old pickup truck was often out of service.

Serving as missionaries meant this inconvenience did not necessarily stop the daily routine. While our daily activities had to be modified because of the frequent mechanical problems, we pressed on to maintain the scheduled services until the repairs could be completed. It often took time to find parts, so having to go without our vehicle could extend for many days.

Our village was surrounded by many other little villages in the mountains. Wild animals such as lions and leopards roamed freely. In addition, our property often was visited with a variety of creatures, including army ants. And a stray dog hung around our place, always begging for a handout. We called him *Fisi*, which means *hyena* in Swahili.

In order to pick up our mail and get some supplies, my wife and I, carrying our daughter, would walk ten kilometers down the mountain when our pickup was out of service. Our trip took us down the dusty, red dirt road that threaded its way along the mountainside. The road ran along the edge of the forest that was often frequented by leopards and other animals. Wild animals often drank from the same spring flowing from the mountainside where we would stop to get a drink.

Because the temperature was cool in the mountains, we needed jackets and carried an umbrella during the rainy season. Returning up the mountain from the village with our mail and supplies one day, a heavy rain began. I nestled our little daughter inside my jacket to keep her warm and dry. My wife walked by my side, holding the umbrella over us the best she could.

The red, dusty road turned into a slippery, muddy mess with numerous mud puddles. Suddenly without warning, my feet went out from under me and I went down, landing in a big puddle of mud and water. I was still holding our daughter with both arms in an effort to protect her. As I got to my feet, I was wet and covered with red mud, soaked to the skin. My wife and I laughed at our circumstances and continued on. Home safely without meeting any leopards this trip, we cleaned up and dried out and prepared for the next day.

One of our routines was to travel every week to the surrounding villages to meet with believers. The local pastors traveled with us. Part of my responsibility was to mentor and be an encouragement by example to these pastors. When our pickup was out of service, Mary and the baby would remain at the mission house, and I would walk to the villages with the pastors. The villages were scattered throughout the surrounding mountains. The circuit to reach all village churches was several kilometers long. Walking the countryside for short distances was something we often did anyway, since petrol (gasoline) was expensive. Adding a few kilometers on foot was not a problem as we were young and energetic.

This was the environment in which we lived and laughed and shared the word of God with our many newfound friends in the mountains of Tanzania. And it was here that the young ministers and I set out on foot early one morning to walk to our villages many miles away. Mary had packed lunches for us, and we were on our way with plans to return by sunset that day. It was a full day of walking, preaching, praying, and sharing God's love throughout the mountains. We needed to get back before dark, if possible.

The Little Dirt Road

At twenty-three years of age, I was full of life and endless energy, and my adventurous spirit and faith allowed me to live fearlessly and push myself to the limits. My love of God and faith in him was all I needed. After all, I was a walking miracle. My life had been spared at birth. I had survived an attack by a rabid dog. I had been raised from a sickbed, unable to walk, as boy. Even so, at twenty-three years of age and full of life, I could still get tired. At the end of this long day, I was ready to return to our little mission house on the mountaintop.

A couple of miles from the mission, we approached a small, mud brick tavern with a grass roof. It was a place where the locals came to drink. The odor of the homemade liquor was very apparent. The smell permeated the air. As we drew nearer, we could hear loud voices coming from inside. The intoxicated people were rowdy and noisy.

Our day had been spent in the distant villages with the local Christians, and we were tired and almost home. A small, mud brick tavern was the last place I felt I would want to enter in an attempt to convert anyone to Christ. I was convinced no one there would want to hear the gospel. But the Lord had instructed us to *"go out into the roads and country lanes and compel them to come in"* (Luke 14:23). Those in the tavern certainly needed to hear about God, but I had one goal in mind for the end of that day—to get back to the little tin house on the mountain where my wife and daughter were awaiting my return. I felt drained and tired from the long day of travel, walking many miles.

Still, it was my responsibility to serve as a model and leader for the young pastors with whom I worked. It was my responsibility to help them become established in their ministry. With my walking stick in my hand, our little band of believers neared the tavern. As we did so, I thought to myself, what were the odds of me influencing or doing something that would change the life of a drunkard?

What I did not realize was that God was preparing me for another opportunity to deepen my understanding of his plan. I recalled the Scripture verse, *"Nevertheless, the one who receives instruction in the word should share all good things with their instructor"* (Galatians 6:6). One who I had instructed in faith was about to become my instructor, for God was molding and shaping all of us on his potter's wheel.

As we were about to pass by the mountain tavern, one of the young ministers looked to me and said, "Pastor, these people need to know about Christ. Let's go in and share the gospel with them." My heart rate

33

suddenly increased, and I am sure my blood pressure also did. I suddenly found myself in a spiritual crisis of my own. How was I going to model leadership in Christian ministry to the young pastors if I told them we should pass on by and leave those people in the dark about the redeeming power of God? On the other hand, I felt that if I walked into that building of intoxicated people, I might not come out alive. My own faith and commitment was once again to face another test. It would have to be by faith alone for me to walk into that place without knowing what the outcome would be.

At the moment I would have felt safer encountering a leopard out in the open than walking in that building. I thought of my wife and daughter waiting for me to come home. I also thought of the many times I had sung, "I'll go where you want me to go, dear Lord." God reminded me of the many times in my past experiences when my faith had brought me through major crises. God was always there with me. The stories of Daniel in the lion's den, the three Hebrew children in the fiery furnace, as well as David facing Goliath all raced through my mind. I was at a fork in the road on my journey of faith. How would I respond, and how would what happened affect my spiritual life and the lives of others?

I was committed, so in faith I turned to the young pastor and said, "If the Spirit of God has shown you we must go in, then we must! Let's go." We walked in, and suddenly a hush fell over the place. The men from the area villages knew us. I felt a tingling sensation race over my body, similar to the time of my healing as a twelve-year-old boy.

The man serving the people the corn liquor was caught off guard and did not know what to say. With his eyes fixed on me, he looked frightened. Not knowing how to react, he dipped an old gourd into the vat of homemade liquor and lifted it up, its foam dripping to the floor. He announced in Swahili, "Welcome, Pastor. Have a drink on me." We stood face to face, looking into each other's eyes. As he held up his gourd filled with liquor, I stood holding up my open Bible.

"What you have to offer me will not satisfy thirst. You will only hide your frustration and obtain false happiness in your desire to escape with your drink. You will end up sick and vomiting and having to return again and again. What I have to offer is the living water where you will never thirst again, where joy and peace will reign in your soul and you will be free." I began to preach, and I challenged all those in the building to come out in the fresh air and listen to what we had to say.

Everyone exited the building and gathered around us on the little dirt road. They sat on the ground in a circle, including the proprietor of the tavern. As I finished sharing what God had given me to say, the young pastors with me began to preach. We witnessed and testified. In time, the men were asked who among them wanted to change their lives and find salvation for their souls. One man who had been in the tavern came forward, weeping. Others sat quietly with heads bowed. The one who came forward found Christ that evening on the little dirt road. We invited all to join us in services.

The following Sunday, the man who had given his heart to the Lord arrived at church smiling. With him was his wife and children. All came to pray and become Christians. He testified how he had sought escape from his troubles and was looking for peace and happiness by drinking. He explained that after he had found the Lord, he had found real peace and happiness in Christ, far beyond what his old lifestyle had offered.

"The Lord is not slow in keeping his promise, as some understand slowness. Instead he is patient with you, not wanting anyone to perish, but everyone to come to repentance." (2 Peter 3:9) I shudder to think of the outcome had I acted on my own human instincts and passed on by. And I am humbled that it was a young pastor and his faith, one whom I was to have been leading, who became my model of obedience that day on the little dirt road. God placed him there to lead me that day.

8

The Book in the Boat

*"Go from your country, your people and your father's household
to the land I will show you."* **Genesis 12:1**

My faith has always included belief that God is like a master painter. We cannot always see the final picture being painted until it is complete. As the artist mixes colors and makes each stroke of the brush, we wait in expectation. In time, on the canvas a beautiful picture is revealed. This story is an analogy as well. At the time we did not understand how a simple book in the bottom of a boat would become a major part of our lives in the future. God, however, was working on the bigger picture, one of us standing before a tribal chief in a distant land.

With so much time available on our long trip at sea that would take us to our first missionary assignment, Mary and I read a lot. After exhausting the supply of reading materials we had brought with us, I asked the captain if there were any other books on board the ship. He told me about a little closet in the engine room where additional books were stored. With instructions on how to locate it, I proceeded below deck.

In the engine room were grated catwalks along the walls, overlooking the noisy, hot engine. The room was steamy with a hot, greasy smell. The crew was busy working. Several little doors on the catwalk led to small rooms along the wall. I was not sure which door was the one for the

Faith Journeys

closet where the books were located, so I asked one of the crew members. He pointed to the door and went on his way.

I was not prepared for what happened next. I did not realize that the rocking of the ship had turned the inside of the closet into a jungle of piled, shifted books. When I opened the door, a cascade of books fell around my feet. I looked down and saw one lying at my feet entitled, *The Lost World of the Kalahari* by Laurens van der Post, an Afrikaner from South Africa. Glancing at the cover, I thought it would be interesting to read. It was about an area of Africa I was not familiar with. I took it back to the cabin and read it.

The book focused on a village called Maun in the Bechuanaland Protectorate, the country later to become known as Botswana. It described the area and told about the people. It spoke of the aborigine tribe of the area, the Bushmen, often referred to as "the harmless people," Africa's last hunter-gatherer people.

The book was fascinating, and I was glad that out of the few hundred books in the closet below deck on the ship, this book had fallen at my feet. Looking back in time, I see this event as orchestrated by God. What were the chances of that specific book falling at my feet at the bottom of a ship in the mid-Atlantic? In my journey of faith, I was learning to rely on the guidance of the Holy Spirit.

Our journey on the African Gulf freighter eventually brought us the continent where we would live and work as missionaries for the next nine years—and return several times over the next fifty years. It was exciting to see land again as we approached the city of Cape Town on the farthest southern tip of Africa. Seals were playing in the harbor, and penguins were walking along the beaches. We were closer to Antarctica than we were home. Over the next weeks, we sailed on to Port Elizabeth, East London, and Durban to unload and load cargo. Then we sailed north in the Indian Ocean to Mozambique, finally reaching our destination of Dar es Salaam, Tanzania.

The port at Dar es Salaam did not have a place for our ship to dock when we arrived, so it was necessary for our freighter to wait a few days in the harbor. The passengers were given the opportunity to go ashore on a small boat or remain on the ship until it could dock. Mary and I decided to go ashore. To do so involved descending down a long, sloping rope-plank walkway hanging on the side of the ship. At the bottom we stepped off into a small boat that was waiting beside the ship. We were taken ashore, where we met the missionary who would transport us to the mission in the mountains.

I forgot about the book I'd retrieved from the engine room in the bottom of the ship. Instead I focused on the work that was ahead of us. After all, the area of Africa written about in the book, the village of Maun, was not our destination. We were located about two thousand miles by road to the north of the area I had read about. We would be working not far from the Kenya border.

We quickly found ourselves very involved in the Tanzania ministry. It was an exciting adventurous time. Above all, it was a great time to serve the Lord and be a part of the Tanzania mission. Our first child, Sally, was born there. Our little tin house in the mountains was our first African home. God was with us and led us through difficult times.

As our one year of ministry commitment in Tanzania came to an end, we awaited the leading of God for our next move. We turned to the Lord for his guidance. The options available to us were to return to the USA and continue our education or remain on the African continent and focus our ministry elsewhere. Returning to the university back home was very tempting, but we had made a great sacrifice to be in Africa for our first year. We had left everything back home. We had raised our funds and had arrived on the continent of Africa.

It was then that God brought the memory of the book I had read a year before back to my mind. The book in the boat again became a part of our lives and fulfillment of the plan of God. It was as if God was speaking to us and letting us know, after our year of service in Tanzania, he was now ready for us to follow him to this village.

Had that book been divinely placed at my feet the year before? As I look back, I can see the hand of God in that event. God was painting the picture, and at our horizon, we could see his divine plan. Our hearts were ready in obedience as we walked by faith into the unknown.

"The gatekeeper opens the gate for him, and the sheep listen to his voice. He calls his own sheep by name and leads them out." **(John 10:3)**

9

The Road South to the Kgotla

"Go south to the road—the desert road." **Acts 8:26**

God showed us the Scripture verse, *"Go south to the road—the desert road"* (Acts 8:26). To actually go the village referred to in the book and begin a ministry would take a miracle. There was much we had to learn on our journey south.

The Canadian group with whom we had been working for our one-year assignment in Tanzania was not registered in the southern part of Africa. We had no legal board to represent us, providing legal documents for entry into the country where we were beginning to feel led to go. We would be facing new languages and a new culture. And we had no place prepared for us if we were to go to there.

What we did not know at the time was, after all the efforts to overcome the obstacles, we would still have to appear before the Kgotla, the council of tribal chiefs. They would have the final say about our working as missionaries in their land. Would God perform a miracle and open the door of ministry to the land we had read about in the book that fell at my feet in the bottom of the boat?

It would certainly be a challenge and a new adventure in faith. At age twenty-four and my wife at age twenty-one, we also had our six-month-old baby to think about and take care of. We would have to live in our truck on the road until we could get established and find accommodations. Being homeless and nomadic would be yet another new experience for us, another test of our commitment.

After making our decision to continue ministry in Africa, we found ourselves ready and excited to journey in faith beyond our next horizon. We were prepared to go where we felt God was leading us. We believed God would to take us, as he did Abraham, to the land he said he would show us (Genesis 12:1). We were challenged by the words recorded in Joshua 1:9, *"Have I not commanded you? Be strong and courageous. Do not be afraid; do not be discouraged, for the LORD your God will be with you wherever you go."*

Numerous obstacles had to be overcome. Approval to work as missionaries in the country had to be obtained. Visas were required. We would have to obtain backing from a registered non-profit organization in the USA. We had no forwarding address for mail except to have our mail sent to general delivery in one of the African cities through which we would pass along the way.

All we had were a few personal possessions, an old military-style Land Rover with over one hundred thousand miles on it, and enough funds to get about halfway to our destination. The journey would be about two thousand miles on gravel roads that were poorly marked, and many rivers had no bridges. We knew we would have to drive through flowing water on several occasions. Logic would dictate the chances of a successful outcome were very low; however, our faith rested on God divinely leading, protecting, and guiding us.

It was late at night when our Land Rover was finally loaded and ready for our trip on the road south. We planned to get some rest and leave early the next morning. The mission house where we had been staying as we prepared to leave was on the slopes of Mount Guong. It towered behind the mission. A big valley lay between us and our only road out. A small river flowed through the valley. A small, meandering dirt road led to a small wooden bridge over the river to the main road. We had built this bridge to replace the last bridge that had washed away in a previous flash flood.

Mountain rains often caused flash floods in the valley, and the chance of the mission bridge washing out was always a concern. Hearing thunder in the distance in the mountains, we felt we needed to start our

The Road South to the Kgotla

journey early and get across the river before morning in case of another flash flood. We were sure we would find a place to rest elsewhere on our trip once we were on our way. After all, we would be spending over a month living in the truck, so how would a few extra hours for an early start make a difference? We decided to begin our journey that night.

We saw the mission disappear in our rearview mirror. We crossed the bridge, leaving our Tanzanian memories behind us. We were on another adventure of faith to the unknown. God was with us, and that was all that mattered.

Not long after we left that night, a flash flood washed the bridge out behind us. With our bridge to the past gone, we began our nomadic life on the road south. In faith, we would live in an old pickup truck until we could acquire accommodations again.

Ahead of us, we still had to descend the mountain to reach the African Rift Valley below us. The torrential rain had created a very hazardous drive on the switch-backed, treacherous dirt road. The risk of sliding off the mountain road was very high, and the valley was hundreds of feet below us. Rushing, muddy water raced down the mountainside, pouring onto the road and off the side. We could be washed off or caught in a landslide at any time.

It became clear that we needed to find a secure place on the mountainside and stop for the night. I found a wide spot in the road and pulled our vehicle close against the high side of the road as far as possible from the drop-off on the other side. In the rain, I placed large rocks around the wheels to secure our vehicle the best I could to minimize the chance of being washed off or sliding over the side. With our vehicle nestled against the dirt bank, we rested.

It was faith and trust in God alone that reassured us we would survive that risky situation. God's hand was on us that lonely night. Thoughts of potential landslides or heavy rains washing us off the road passed through our minds, but we dismissed the thoughts. God had made it clear that we were to *go south to the road—the desert road* (Acts 8:26) and beyond *"to the land I will show you"* (Genesis 12:1).

I was reminded of the disciples in the boat in the storm. Jesus had clearly said when he got in the boat, *"Go over to the other side"* (Mark 4:35). Would Jesus have said this if the boat were going to sink? Likewise, would Jesus have told us go south to Botswana and then allow us to be washed off the side of a mountain? In the peaceful arms of God, we rested on the mountainside in the storm until morning.

As the sun rose, a new day in our ministry was beginning. We were out of communication with everyone back home. We had arranged for our mail to be forwarded to general delivery in a city we would pass through on our way south. We were homeless, a nomadic couple with a six-month-old baby, living in an old truck. We were happy, however, for we were in the will of the Lord.

After the rain, we descended the mountain, forded the river in the valley below, and began our long journey. We camped, cooked, and lived along the road, washing clothes in rivers and drying them on scrub brush bushes and rocks. We slept in the back of our pickup that had a canvas tarp over pipe racks. Along the way, we encountered troops of monkeys that tried to steal our food. Baboons would greet us at times, as well as other wild animals. God was with us always.

We arrived in the city of Bulawayo, Zimbabwe, after traveling through Zambia. We had no place to go. At night we slept in a small city park. We picked up our mail from general delivery at the post office, and we were able to reestablish communications by mail with people back home. We found a bank that would process our checks so we would have funds to continue our journey. As we cooked our meals and lived in the park, we began to plan our next move.

After about a month, some British Christians found us and invited us to their mission church. Our new friends introduced us to an elderly British lady. We were able to rent an old garage behind her house that had been converted into a simple living quarters. While we lived in the garage, we organized our final entry into the Bechuanaland Protectorate, now called Botswana. We still had a few hundred miles to go.

That little garage was a comfortable, clean, safe shelter for which we were grateful after living on the road and in a park for many weeks. God had brought us this far, but we still needed one more miracle to complete our journey to "the lost world of the Kalahari." God gave us this verse to assure us of his leading. *The LORD himself goes before you and will be with you; he will never leave you nor forsake you. Do not be afraid; do not be discouraged"* (Deuteronomy 31:8).

We had reached the most southern point in our journey. It was now time for us to travel northwest to reach the village of Maun. We were

The Road South to the Kgotla

not at our final destination but well on our way. Our journey of faith would still take us over more hurdles before we reached the goal God had placed over our horizon.

Our three months of living in our truck and then a garage had gone by fast, but we were now better prepared. The Christian friends God had given us in Zimbabwe had been very helpful. We'd had the opportunity to preach and share the gospel with the people in their country. We were now ready to cross the Kalahari Desert in our journey to Maun. It was going to be a radical change from the beautiful mountains of Tanzania. We were headed for the Kgotla.

We were able to purchase a small utility trailer, and we loaded it with our few belongings along with enough supplies for survival. The back of our Land Rover pickup, with its metal racks and a tarp cover, would be our only home once again. Each night we would place our baby's grass basket bed, which the Tanzanian Christians had made for us, in the back of the truck. Supplies and equipment were packed on the sides, leaving just enough room on each side of the basket for us to sleep.

We did not know how long this living arrangement would be, but we were prepared until we could find a place to live. We had become used to living in the truck, so were prepared for this part of our journey. The road lay before us, inviting us to begin.

We had no guarantee that we would be permitted to conduct missionary work in Botswana as we left Zimbabwe; however, our adventurous faith kept us focused, and we pressed toward the goal we believed God had set before us. Like a runner jumping hurtles, our journey of faith was leading us continually forward, over each hurtle that lay before us.

Our route to Maun began on a narrow gravel road that crossed a wide riverbed. There was no bridge, and many times in the arid bush country, the nearly dry river was subject to flash flooding during the rainy season. To be prepared, we had equipped our vehicle with extension vertical exhaust pipes and seal coated the wiring for water crossings when necessary. Over the years, we would become very familiar with this dry river bed, for we would have to cross it many times when the water level was high and dangerous. At times we would have to set camp and wait for the water to recede.

The trip to our destination in Maun was too far to complete in a day, so we stopped near a small village by a river and set up camp for

Faith Journeys

the night. There was enough scrub brush and small trees to provide sufficient firewood for our camp and a limited supply of water. As the sun set, we prepared our evening meal. In the light of the campfire, we could see scorpions scampering around with their stinger tails high in the air. We were becoming accustomed to these critters and wary of them as well. They were dangerous and could deliver an extremely painful sting.

A small group of bright eyed, smiling children arrived at our camp that night. They had seen our campfire and came from the nearby village to visit us. They stood a few yards away, grinning at us with their small spears in their hands. They were too poor to afford clothes, so they had only loincloth to wear. We welcomed them to share our meal with us.

The children, we learned, had no school to attend, but they understood survival and had a lot they could teach us. God's love flowed through us as our hearts went out to these precious little children. We had come to their country to live among them and share the love of God with them and their families.

Our camp was in lion country, and many other wild animals and creatures roamed the countryside freely. Snakes such as pythons large enough to kill young cattle were in the bush. Hooded cobras and black mamba snakes moved around freely. After dinner and some time with the children, we made preparations to sleep. With our little daughter tucked safely in her grass basket in the back of the truck, we crawled in, pulling a light blanket over us to keep out the chill of the cool, desert night.

In the early hours of the morning, we heard a noise at the back of our truck. The scratching sound alerted us that something was attempting to enter where we were sleeping. Again we heard the sound, and our blanket slowly moved down. We were used to unexpected challenges so did not panic. In bush country in Africa, we'd learned to face each event with faith in God. We knew God was in control of everything, including potentially dangerous creatures. Did not God control the lions in the den with Daniel? We were living among the lions that roamed the countryside freely.

I carefully considered my response to our night visitor. We had nothing with which to defend ourselves, so all I could do was attempt to surprise the potential intruder. Was it a python, or maybe a lion? How would the perpetrator respond? We definitely knew there was something there; the noise continued, and our blanket kept slowly moving off us.

The Road South to the Kgotla

I quietly told Mary I would attempt to frighten the perpetrator. I sat up, with my flashlight in hand, and quickly lit up the back of the truck, letting out a loud, growling noise. In the beam of my light was a goat, both hoofs resting on the tailgate, as he ate the blanket right off our backs. He had apparently missed out on our evening meal, so he'd come by for late night stack. I guessed he was from the nearby village.

Mary and I laughed and thanked God for being there for us, even when our faith and trust in him was continually challenged by unexpected experiences. We rested peacefully for the remainder of the night, knowing lions would not bother us when they had a crazy goat roaming around for their evening meal. Besides, our God had delivered us many times before. He had miraculously guided our lives this far. He was our God on the mountain, and we knew he was the God of our valleys.

We finally arrived at our destination, the village of Maun, home to ten thousand people. As we drove into the village at dusk, the smoke of thousands of fires rose slowly over the village. The people were preparing their evening meals. In every direction, we could see the seeming endless number of small, round, mud homes with grass roofs. The chatter of children could be heard everywhere.

God had told us to *"leave your country and your people, and go to the land I will show you"* (Acts 7:3). We had arrived. We had completed yet another portion of our faith journey, the one that began when the Lord said to us, *"Go south to the road—the desert road"* (Acts 8:26). It seemed like a long journey from the time I had found and read the book in the boat about this area and its people to where we were this evening. Once again I recognized it was by divine intervention that God had brought us here.

We had one final hurtle to cross. We wanted to establish our ministry in tribal land, and the tribal chiefs had jurisdiction about all matters that involved their people. We had to go to the tribal chiefs to obtain permission to live among them and share the gospel among their people. We had to arrange a meeting with the chiefs of the area.

In the center of the village was a large tree in a clearing where all of the area chiefs would meet to discuss the affairs of their community. This place was called the Kgotla, pronounced (*coat-lah*) in the Tswana language. It was a public meeting place as well as the traditional law court of a Botswana village. The Maun village Kgotla was led by Chief Moremi, the wife of the previous chief, who had died.. Community decisions at the Kgotla were always arrived at by consensus. We made arrangements to appear before the elders at the Kgotla to request permission to become a part of their community and follow our call of the Lord. The elders and the chief would have the final say, and we would have to respect their decision.

We arrived at the Kgotla on the morning of our meeting. Standing before Chief Moremi and the district's elderly chiefs was a twenty-four-year-old Indiana boy who, by faith, had come this far. At his side stood his wife, Mary, at twenty-two, who had grown up very poor. In her arms was our little blond-haired baby daughter, Sally.

We politely shared our vision with the chiefs and explained that God had brought us to their land to live among them and share the good news of Christ. We shared our hearts, allowing the Spirit of God to direct each word. They asked us many questions to which we responded. One important question they asked was what additional activities we were planning.

Being aware that the illiteracy rate there was over 90 percent at the time because of lack of schools, we told them we would establish an adult literacy program as a part of our ministry. To commit to an adult literacy program in a land where we barely knew the language would be a challenge; however, in faith we felt it could be achieved. We knew it was important for the people to be able to read the Word of God for themselves. After sharing our hearts at the Kgotla, we were dismissed by the elders and informed that they would discuss the matter among themselves and would let us know of their decision. We left and waited for their answer.

Had God brought us this far only to be refused? If they were to say no, we had no place to go. We needed a miracle. We had come this far by faith. We waited, having a deep-seated peace that God was with us and had opened door after door, leading us this far.

The country of Botswana was a protectorate managed by the British government. The internal affairs were managed by the chiefs, while the British government provided security and protection for the people. A British District Commissioner represented the tribal chiefs. The tribal chiefs were to share their decision with him, and he would inform us of their decision.

The next day, we saw the District Commissioner approaching us. He smiled and our hearts leaped. This was certainly a good sign. "The Kgotla has given approval for you to live and work among their people," he said. Our hearts were filled with joy as we praised the Lord. Our journey of faith to this place had been successful. Excitement and enthusiasm

The Road South to the Kgotla

rushed through our minds. We were anxious to get started in the work ahead of us.

I asked the wise, elderly British District Commissioner about how to acquire land so we could get started. He smiled and said, "Son, why don't you start out like your boss. In time, if you need land, we will deal with that." Puzzled, I asked what he meant by "your boss." "Did Jesus have land and buildings?" he replied. I understood what he was saying, so I smiled and thanked him, and we went our way rejoicing.

Excited that God had opened the door, I sent a telegram home that simply stated, *"I have placed before you an open door that no one can shut."* (Revelation 3:8). We knew God had opened the door before us. We were prepared to walk through the door and share the redemption story of Christ.

Our ministry to the people of Botswana started under a tree without a building or land. Today there are church buildings and Christians in many communities in the area. God led us to a Christian woman named Tsidiso. A very well educated lady, she, being bilingual, became Mary's assistant. She attended our first service under the tree. With our resources and her skills, an adult literacy program began. It was so successful that the Botswana government allowed us to select a representative from our mission for special international training in Israel. Tsidiso, the founder of the mission's literacy program, now serves as the Botswana National leader of the mission.

We are now several generations away from that first service under a tree. The little children of those days are now the elders, grandparents, and great-grandparents of the continually growing church. The young adults of the church are now lawyers, pilots, bankers, teachers, surveyors, nurses, and pastors. The seed that was planted grew, and the church has become a big influence in the country. The church is alive and well, strong and growing.

As the sun sets on one generation, the dawn of a new day is arriving for the next. In the journey of faith, God is always there with all who will believe and walk with eternal values in view. It was a journey of faith from the book in Mid-Atlantic to the Kgotla. God saw the finished picture long before, just as he continues to see what is over each of our horizons.

God performed a miracle at the Kgotla. Jesus said, *"On this rock I will build my church, and the gates of Hades will not overcome it."* (Matthew 16:18)

10

The Blind Man

"You guide me with your counsel, and afterward you will take me into glory." **Psalm 73:24**

The tree in Maun where we began preaching and sharing the gospel outdoors was located on tribal land, and since no one was using it, we had permission to gather there. Logs were cut and laid on the ground to provide a place for people to sit. In time the people cut enough limbs to create a brush arbor. It kept free-roaming cattle out and gave a nice area where we could conduct regularly scheduled services. The people loved to come and worship God under the tree. Our congregation began to grow, but we never forgot the children who came to us first, on the road south to this land.

God uses children in a special way to touch the hearts of adults. The children of Botswana were taught at an early age to hold their elders in high respect. It was not uncommon to see children happily assisting the older population. This was the case of the blind man.

It was not long before our small band of believers had become a large enough group that they wanted to erect their first church building. It was their tribal land, so they arranged with the tribal chiefs to build it by the tree where the mission began. The Botswana Christians were the Botswana church, so we encouraged their full involvement from the beginning. They designed, planned, and constructed their building on their land.

To Western standards the first church building would be considered primitive, but to the faithful group of Botswana Christians, it was a beautiful place to worship God. It sat on a knoll at the edge of the village with a wide, open, sandy area in front. Its frame was made of poles cut from trees. The bark of the trees was stripped off and used to tie the poles together. Reeds from the river were used for walls, and grass was woven to cover the structure. The logs that had been used for seating in the brush arbor were placed on the mud and cow dung floor of that beautiful, little building.

Many families came to the services. Present, also, were lots of children and young people. When it was time for service, I would ring the church bell, which was a flat metal part of a broken truck spring that we would hit with a tire lever. It made a clear ringing sound that could be heard throughout the village.

One Sunday morning I looked out toward the village and saw a small group of children walking toward the church. In the middle of the group was a tall, stately man. It became apparent that the children were leading a man who was blind. One young boy was holding onto the end of the man's walking stick. The other children cleared twigs and rocks from his path and kept watch for dangerous snakes. The children of Botswana had great respect for the elderly. As they led the blind man into the church, everyone welcomed him.

When the blind man learned about how God loved him and that Jesus came to bring him salvation, he became a believer. He was thrilled, and he thanked the children who had taken the time to invite him and bring him to the service. He started attending faithfully. After hearing a message about baptism, he wanted to be baptized.

Baptism was a big event at the church, and everyone, including visitors from the community, would come. On the day of the baptism service, everyone gathered at the river with the blind man. He was filled with joy to be able to participate in the service. Everyone watched as he was led to the edge of the water. The little children who had first brought him to church were there.

When I took his hand, prepared to lead him into the water, he asked to speak. He began by telling the people on the riverbank that he was

The Blind Man

blind. He said that in faith, he had relied on the children to lead him to the church. He explained how he had wanted to hear about God and be able to know him. He said that in faith, he believed the words he had heard, so he gave his heart to God. He then explained how he had learned about baptism, so he wanted to be obedient and be baptized.

"I grew up here," he said, "and I know the river. There are pythons around that could kill me. There are crocodiles in the river that could attack me. I stand here now on the banks of this river. I have followed God in faith. I have placed my trust in those who shared the gospel with me. Now, as a blind man, I place my life in the hands of my pastor, who will baptize me in this river. I go into the water with faith in God, who saved my soul."

Many lives were changed the day the blind man, led by the children, followed the Lord in baptism. Each of us has an influence on others. Our faith can touch the lives of many, igniting the flame of faith in their hearts. The journey of faith continues from generation to generation, nurtured by our faith-building life experiences and the sharing of stories of the past.

11

The Sick Woman

"Assemble the people before me to hear my words so that they may learn to revere me as long as they live in the land and may teach them to their children." **Deuteronomy 4:10**

Mary led the children's ministry, and I taught the adults in the early days at the mission church in Botswana. Mary taught the children about how Jesus healed people. She explained that he was the Son of God, and he came to save us from our sins. The children loved the Bible stories Mary taught them and loved to share them with others as well.

One Sunday morning when it was time for the service, a woman from the village arrived whom we had not met before. People from the village would often come to visit the services for the first time. It was always good to see new people come, and the congregation and Mary and I would always welcome them.

By this time, we had been able to purchase some benches for the people to sit on, replacing the logs we had used at the beginning. She was welcomed, and sat down. After the opening of the service, visitors were asked if they had anything to share. The visiting woman stood up and began to speak.

She said she had been very ill for several months. It seemed in spite of everything she did, her health problem continued to become worse. She told us how discouraged she had become. She went on to say that a group of children from the mission had stopped by her house. She said they lived nearby her and knew about her illness, so they had come to visit her.

The woman explained that the children told her about Jesus and what they had learned at the mission. They told her God loved her and wanted to heal her, and they gathered around her and prayed for her. She said something happened to her when the children prayed, and she felt the power of God. She was healed.

"I came to the mission to find out what was happening here," she said. She proceeded to say that the faith of those little children was amazing to her, that she needed that kind of faith in her life. That morning she gave her heart to God and became a believer.

It has been exciting to watch the journey of faith of those children. Today they are grandparents, working in the church and pointing the way for the next generation to follow.

12

Powdered Milk

"He provides food for those who fear him; he remembers his covenant forever." **Psalm 111:5**

Sally was about a year and a half old when our second daughter, Sara, arrived. Sally was happy to have a baby sister. Around that same time, we became aware of some orphaned children in the village who needed a home. Our hearts went out to them. Two of these little children, named David and Bambi, and an orphaned teen named Gloria came to live with us, so we became a family of seven overnight. To ensure good development of health for the children, we needed a good food supply, especially milk, which was often hard to find.

The ministry in Botswana had been established for some time, and our daily schedule was very full. Many people had become Christians, and the church was growing. Mary and I labored continually, serving the people and sharing the love of God. We had several regularly scheduled services and Bible studies throughout the week. More villages had been added to our ministry. Buildings were being erected, and God was blessing our labors.

In addition to our adult literacy program, we had added several other ministries to help the people. Mary was teaching classes in cooking, knitting, and other life skills, while I taught mechanics and building skills and gave driving lessons. I fished and hunted with the people as well. Once I was with the local people tracking a lion that had been killing their cattle. Our only weapons while walking through the tall grass were spears.

Our mission church had become like a big family, with our many new brothers and sisters in Christ. We shared and cared for one another and were encouraged by each other's faith. While Mary and I shared the gospel and our skills with the people, they taught us how to thatch roofs, survival techniques, and above all, patience, love, and long-suffering. We were blessed.

The survival techniques we learned from the people amazed and blessed us as our family was established and growing. Our second daughter, Sara, was born at the village hospital of Maun. The hospital was on the banks of the Thamalakane River, where crocodiles and pythons roamed freely. Lions, elephants, and other big game were always nearby. When a mother cat delivered a litter of kittens at the mission, the hospital staff asked us if they could have the kittens. We asked why, and they explained that the cats were good at keeping the cobras out of the hospital.

Obtaining milk for our children was difficult. There was no fresh milk available, so we had learned to use powered milk to provide the necessary protein nourishment. The powdered milk came in cans shipped from England. Generally we were able to purchase this milk locally at a small general store.

When our supply of powdered milk began to dwindle, I went as usual to purchase more but found the supply in the store was sold out. Not only that, but the store owners could not assure me when more powdered milk would arrive. They informed me they were waiting for the overland transport truck to bring it from across the Kalahari Desert.

As our supply became dangerously low, I continued trying to find milk for the children. None was available anywhere in the village. One morning we took the final traces of powdered milk out of the bottom of the can and fixed milk for the children. We knew the kids would survive without milk, but living in such a hostile environment with so many diseases, we wanted to be sure the children were well nourished to maintain their health. We needed a miracle.

We still had a small supply of the rainwater we had collected from the metal roof of the mission house during the rainy season. We would

Powdered Milk

have to ration it. We also had water from the river that was available. River water, however, had to be boiled well to destroy the many parasites and other bacteria. The water from the river was known to be infested with the parasite Schistosomiasis (Bilharzia).

We remembered that God's Word said all our needs would be supplied according to his riches in glory. Would God supply powered milk for the children? We had learned to live our lives with our faith on autopilot, not demanding things from God but living with simple faith and trust that God would be with us and meet our needs.

I was reminded how Elijah told the widow woman to take the last of the flour and prepare a meal. The Scriptures say, "*For the jar of flour was not used up and the jug of oil did not run dry, in keeping with the word of the LORD spoken by Elijah*" (1 Kings 17:16). I remembered also how Jesus took the five loaves and two fish and fed thousands. Could God possibly supply more milk for our children when none was available locally?

On the day we emptied the milk can, using the last of the powdered milk, we continued with our daily routine as usual. The children had their needs met for the morning. That day just *happened* to be the same day the mail plane was to arrive. It was usually mid-morning when we would hear sounds of the twin engine DC-3 coming from the east.

The sun, reflecting off our corrugated metal roof on the mission house, had become the beacon for arriving planes. They would fly over the mission house and make a turn, descending toward the grass airstrip for a landing. The sound of the approach gave us enough time to drive to the airfield in our four-wheel-drive vehicle.

Of our several ministries, one was providing used clothing for people in our village who could not afford clothing. Many children would attend church with nothing more to wear than a loincloth, and no one was ever turned away. The used clothing, however, was always a blessing, and the families were thankful to receive it. To enable this ministry, congregations back home in the USA would prepare boxes of used clothing and ship them to us. It would often take up to three months from the time a box was mailed for it to arrive at the mission via plane.

As the plane rolled to a stop and we arrived at the airstrip, the people began to unload the cargo. A crate of fresh fruit and other supplies from Zimbabwe arrived with our family's mail. There was also another box that had been sent from the USA by a congregation in Oklahoma. That church had faithfully supported our efforts from the beginning of our ministry. I picked up our mail and the boxes and returned to the mission.

Mail days were always a time of excitement. When I arrived back at the mission, we would check the mail for news from home and for support checks to see if we would be able to meet the month's budget. Tasting some of the fresh fruit from the adjacent country was always refreshing. The boxes from the congregations back home would then be opened and the clothing sorted.

The box from Oklahoma that arrived on the plane had been postmarked three months before. As we began to take the used clothing out of the box, we felt something in the bottom. We lifted off the clothing, and there below it was the largest box of powdered milk we had ever seen. A simple note was taped to the top of the box of milk that read, "Thought you might need this."

Keep in mind, this box had been shipped three months before we needed it. It arrived the exact morning that our powdered milk had run out. The people who sent it had no clue that we would need the powdered milk on that day. Even we did not know we would run out of milk on that date three months before this package was shipped.

In over fifty years of ministry, traveling and working in several countries, never before nor since has anyone ever shipped us a box of powdered milk!

We serve an all-knowing God. We serve a God of all circumstances. From time to time in our journey of faith, God, in unique ways, performs miracles to honor our faith. God wants to reassure us of his presence. And God gives us experiences and stories to share with others for their encouragement. The Christians in Oklahoma put the powdered milk in the box in faith and obedience as God showed them to do. Their faith and our faith were honored that day when the plane landed.

13

The Village Reader

"She did what she could." **Mark 14:8**

The village of Maun in the Republic of Botswana was located on the edge of the Okavango Delta. The Delta is the end of a large river that flows out of Angola. In this region are many remote, isolated villages. It was in one of these remote villages that we first met the young woman I call the village reader.

In the early 1960s, maps of the area were scarce. However, Hitler and the German Axis had controlled the territory adjacent to our area in that part of Africa. They had systematically produced aeronautical maps with flights over the area in anticipation of expanding their territory. I was able to obtain a copy of an old World War II German aeronautical map of the region where the mission was located.

The map was reasonably accurate, and in studying it, I saw several villages surrounding Maun. The map showed them as large clusters of round, mud brick homes with grass roofs. There were no roads to these villages. The only way into them was to walk or go by donkey. They were very isolated and had names with unusual sounds such as *Xaixai* and *Xgaraxlau*. The proper pronunciation included clicking sounds. As an example, the village of Xaixai would be pronounced *Kah-he-kah-he* with a clicking sound accompanying the letter *k* included. *Xgaraxlau* was the name of another village, pronounced *Kah-rock-laoh* with a clicking sound on the letter *k*.

In those days the villagers used sand sleighs to transport goods from place to place. The sand sleigh was made from a large, forked tree trunk. Flat on its side, the trunk formed the letter *V*, which became runners. Slats were attached to the top of the flat V with post rails along the sides. The sand sleigh was then pulled by a donkey that would meander through and around trees, creating miles of narrow, winding, sandy trails. Our first trips to the villages surrounding Maun were by foot on trails made by sand sleighs.

Mary and I were among the first foreigners to visit in some of these villages. We would often find the villages empty, the people fearing who we were. In time, however, we developed relationships with the people who lived there, and we began regular visits to help and encourage them. Eventually we were able clear enough trees to get our four-wheel-drive Land Rover in and out. It was in this setting that we found the village reader. She was a beautiful child of God, having become a believer as a young girl.

The Western world places a lot of emphasis on beauty. Television commercials certainly reflect this fact of our culture. Beauty pageants determine who the most beautiful woman is. Standards and guidelines are set to determine beauty. Beauty, however, is relative; it can be seen in other ways.

At this point in the story, most readers form a visual image of a young woman who may have looked like Pocahontas. The beauty of this woman, however, was not how she looked, but who she was. Her beauty was from the Spirit within her broken body. In spite of her condition, her eyes sparkled, and the smile of her distorted face radiated the very presence of God's love.

This servant of God had been the victim of leprosy and was extremely disfigured. Her face was so disfigured that she did not have an unblemished area on her skin. It was crumpled and lumpy. Her arms, hands, and feet were the same; her fingers and toes were gone. When we first met her, she was dressed in ragged clothes and was barefoot.

Because of leprosy, as a young child the village reader had been able to live in a leprosy colony. She learned to read at the facility. She also learned about Christ and became a believer. The Spirit of God flowing out from her life was felt whenever anyone was in her presence. God had placed her in this village, and after we met her, in the ministry of the mission, for such as time as this. She was God sent.

This young disfigured woman, never complaining, was a faithful servant of God. Her testimony rang out in the village from her kind voice whenever she spoke. Though her journey of faith had taken her down a difficult road, she was a woman of great faith and a great influence on our lives. Each week as we traveled to the village, our Christian friend would always be waiting for us. When we arrived, she would meet us with a big smile on her face. She was a dedicated worker and servant of the Lord.

Bibles in the Tswana language were scarce, but we were able to obtain enough to give out to the few who were able to read. The village reader was the only one in her area who had received the opportunity to learn to read, so she kept the village Bible. Throughout the week, she would gather the people and read to them. It was with great difficulty that she balanced the Bible on the stub of her hand with no fingers. She used the palm of her other hand to flip the pages to find the Scriptures. Her testimony and impact on the village was phenomenal. She led many people to the Lord.

We lived and ministered in Botswana for seven years. Since it was the country where our second daughter, Sara, was born, joining Sally, who was about a year and a half old when Sara was born, it was the only home these two children knew. When our work was finished in Botswana, we went to Latin America to minister. Years later, we were able to return to Africa. We would spend our summers in Botswana, working along with the church. We were able to travel to many of the villages where we had ministered before. It was always good to be home in Africa again. We had the opportunity to meet the many new believers, and always looked forward to visiting with our old friends.

One summer when we returned, we did not see the village reader, so I inquired about her. We learned that she had moved to another village, so we made a special trip in a remote area to locate her. On arrival, she saw us and came running toward us with the same big smile as before and gave us a big hug. While much older, her eyes still sparkled.

She was living in a very small village with a few families. She took us by the hand and led us to her little mud house, proudly pointing to a sign she had placed over her door. It had been painted very crudely with

Faith Journeys

bristles of a broken stick that had been hammered by a rock to expose the fibers. There were no available brushes where she lived, so it was all she had available to make the sign. The sign read, *"Phutego ya Modimo,"* meaning the place where the people of God gather.

Our friend explained to us that the Bible says, *"Where two or three are gathered together in my name, there am I in the midst of them."* (Matthew 18:20, KJV) She said she gathered the children and adults of the area together each week and taught them about Jesus, reading the Bible. "We are God's family in this village," she explained. Her faith was phenomenal. Our faith was strengthened by her presence.

On a recent visit to her area, we learned she had gone on to be with the Lord. Her journey of faith has taken her beyond the horizon into the presence of God her Creator. Certainly she has a special place in heaven. Her faithfulness was an inspiration to many. She helped us understand commitment and faithfulness, regardless of the circumstances of life. Her story reminds me that God paints a beautiful picture one brushstroke at a time.

14

Math Miracle

"The little you had before I came has increased, and the Lord has blessed you wherever I have been. But now, when may I do something for my own household?" **Genesis 30:30**

As our ministry in Botswana expanded, it became apparent we would need to construct additional facilities to carry out the many operations. The mission was located in the northwest corner of Botswana, so supplies had to be transported across the Kalahari Desert, a few hundred miles from the nearest rail line. We wondered, what kind of miracle would need to happen in order for us to have what we needed to construct the additional facilities?

In faith we chose to build with brick because we wanted the buildings to last for many years. This decision, however, presented many challenges. Where would we obtain the bricks? How would we construct the brick buildings? And I was certainly not a bricklayer.

Our family's livelihood was based on donations sent in faith from the USA. We wanted to invest wisely as good stewards of the funds with which God had entrusted us. As a result, we lived very practical lives. We prepared to meet the developing challenges in faith that God would be with us to obtain the goal.

65

We had recently received a gasoline-powered wringer washing machine shipped to us from the USA. It was a great timesaver, replacing the washboard and tub we had been using, though it was still necessary for us to heat our water in a fifty-five gallon drum over a wood fire. As I dismantled the wood crate used to ship the washer, I saved each board and straightened every nail, thinking they would certainly come in handy during construction. These items were difficult to obtain locally and were high priced. We lived with the philosophy of "waste not, want not."

We had a couple of small hardware stores in the village. When the time came to purchase the construction materials, I went there and asked the shopkeepers where I could buy bricks. They laughed and said there were no bricks available. One said, "If you want bricks, you make bricks."

I was not beyond making bricks. Hard work had never been a problem for me, so making bricks would be easy. I asked the storekeeper, "If I make the bricks, where can I obtain a brick mold?"

Again he laughed and said, "If you want a brick mold, you make it." I knew what course of action I would have to take. We had to be resourceful and figure out how to solve our own problems.

Computers, search engines, bookstores, libraries, or other information resources were not available where we were and at this time. Our life in the Okavango Delta in the early 1960s was similar to the way it was in the early days in America. We were isolated from the rest of the world, with limited contact capabilities. The only up-to-date news we received came by short wave radio. Even then, when the batteries failed, it could take weeks to get more. Mail took several weeks to arrive. I would have to rely on my own thoughts and God for how to make the brick mold and the bricks.

Returning from the hardware store, I took the wood and straightened nails from the wood crate used to ship the gasoline-powered wringer washing machine, and I made brick molds. Together with the local Christians, we dug a pit near the river where there was a source of clay. We carried water in buckets from the river to pour into the clay pit. We mixed the mud and water in the pit using our bare feet, similar to how the Hebrews did in Egypt when they made bricks.

Using the mud we'd made, we formed the bricks in the molds. We then sun-dried the bricks, rotating them periodically. Next we built a

Math Miracle

kiln and gathered firewood. Over time, we made and fired over thirty thousand bricks! We designed our buildings, staked out the sites, and prepared to build the structures we needed using our mud bricks.

I always looked to the Lord for guidance on every phase of a project. It was something I had tried to do all my life. I began experimenting with possible patterns for laying the bricks. At last I settled on a pattern I felt the Lord had shown me. I did not have an official name for the pattern, but it made sense to me. I felt that God had honored my faith and trust in him to supply the logic and understanding I needed. We were ready, I thought, to build a new church building, a mission house, storage buildings, and classrooms.

It was our policy, as much as was possible, not to generate debts. Our ministry was conducted totally by faith. A standing contract arrangement with a guaranteed income would have been nice, but we had none. We were totally dependent on God to supply our needs. In faith with the resources on hand, we completed laying bricks and finished all the walls of the mission building. We were ready to install the roof trusses and metal roof.

The rainy season was quickly approaching, so we needed to complete the roof before the rains set in. We had exhausted our funds, so I felt we had no choice in this case but to charge the required materials. We did so, believing that somehow God would intervene and meet our need before the bills came due.

It was exciting when we finished the mission building ahead of the rains, but we had a debt of two thousand dollars. The due date was fast approaching. Two thousand dollars was a lot of money in the 1960s. God was about to honor our faith and perform a miracle that defied explanation.

Our support came in small amounts such as fifteen or twenty dollars at a time from individuals and congregations scattered all over the USA. There was no coordination or communicated networks to ensure we would receive a specific amount. People, by faith, gave as they felt led by the Spirit of God. Their donations were mailed to us in Africa directly from the USA. It would take a month or more for a letter and donation to reach us. Normally a few donations would trickle in each week. The day our debt of two thousand dollars was due was also the day the mail plane was due to arrive.

Faith Journeys

On Monday, before the due date of our bill on Thursday, Mary and I discussed the matter. We had absolutely no assurance that the money would be available to pay the bill, but deep down in our hearts, we knew we served a God who was aware of our need and was with us in all circumstances. We felt a peace that God would meet our need. God had been with us over and over again. He had led us, guided us, and healed us. He had protected and provided for us.

We tried never to make irresponsible, unreasonable demands for God to help us. In simple faith, we knew that he knew our needs, and that was all we needed to know. We lived knowing God understood and was with us and knew our situation. We were his servants, and this was his ministry. Mary and I felt somehow God would supply. We rested in the assurance that he would meet our need. We had not forgotten his recent provision of powdered milk.

As the mail plane rolled to a stop the day our bill was due, little did we know what was about to happen. The mailbag on the plane was packed with letters from all over the USA. They came from the West Coast, from the East Coast, from the North, and from the South. Each had been mailed individually several weeks before the bill was due. All had arrived on the specific day of our need.

As we opened each letter, we began to add the amounts of the enclosed donations. Fifteen dollars here, fifty dollars there. We counted and totaled the amount. It came to exactly $2,021.

We laughed, we cried, we rejoiced. Once again, God had met our need just in time. Mary then said, "I wonder what the twenty-one dollars is for?" I replied, "Pressed down, full, and running over, as the Scripture says, I suppose. Three times seven is twenty-one. Perhaps God just wanted us to know it was from him."

With no computers and no interactive communication, weeks before the deadline for our bill, the Spirit of God had moved among his people. They responded to his voice in faith. He would tell one individual to send a check for a given amount and mail it that day. Another day he would speak to someone else to put a check into the mail.

The West Coast donations had to be posted earlier to link up and arrive with the East Coast donations. The Spirit of God was calculating the amount, and he knew whom to call on to donate. He knew how much each needed to donate, and he knew when each one should send it so it

Math Miracle

would arrive the day of the need. Every part of this event had been coordinated by God, who saw us and blessed us in our journey of faith.

God performed a math miracle that day. As with the story of the powdered milk, never before had such an event happened and never since then did it happen in all of our fifty years of ministry overseas. But on that day, God honored the faith of his people and provided a miracle.

It was years later, when we were back in the USA, that I learned the pattern I had used for laying the bricks had a name. It was called *Flemish Bond*, said to be the most ideal method for use in that area and for that type of construction. As I write, the buildings built those years ago still stand. And the little brick church is now the oldest standing church building still in use in the community of Maun, Botswana, the village at the end of the road south.

Part II

African Snake Encounters and God's Protecting Hand

15

The Cobra in the Field

"If you do not stand firm in your faith, you will not stand at all." **Isaiah 7:9**

"He led you through the vast and dreadful wilderness, that thirsty and waterless land, with its venomous snakes and scorpions. He brought you water out of hard rock." **Deuteronomy 8:15**

Oftentimes in our journey of faith, we encounter the unexpected. Economic crises, physical crises, broken relationships can often cascade on us without warning. I want to share an experience I had in a remote part of the backcountry of Botswana, Africa, in the 1960s when numerous venomous snakes were plentiful and encountered frequently. This encounter was short-lived, but the point of the story lives on.

I was walking through dry shrub brush when I came upon a hooded cobra. It had coiled in preparation to strike, and I was only a couple of steps away from it. I stopped in my tracks and did not move a muscle. I wanted to diminish any further threat to the snake. Any movement on my part could easily initiate a strike by the cobra.

Faith Journeys

We were in a standoff. It would not un-coil for fear I would attack it, so it remained ready to strike. My choice of action was limited as well. If I turned to run, the action might cause the snake to strike.

I had learned years before that God is in control of all circumstances, so I placed the matter in the hands of my Creator. My prayer was simple and short. "Lord, you sent me here to serve you. This cobra is your creation, and I place this matter in your hands." I looked down as the cobra uncoiled and crawled away. I continued on my way.

Some may say the encounter would have ended in this way without my praying to God. It may have been, they would say, just a coincidence. I, however, will always be convinced that it was an example of divine intervention and perhaps a test of my faith. I believe God gave me the instinct to freeze in my tracks. The divine interaction brought resolution to the crisis.

Oftentimes believers encounter evil without warning. The forces of evil may appear ready to strike and destroy. In the journey of faith, preparation must be made so that no matter what happens in life, we will be ready and able to stand strong. God gives us this ability when we arm ourselves with faith and trust. The apostle Paul wrote in Ephesians 6:13–14, *"Therefore, put on the full armor of God, so that when the day of evil comes, you may be able to stand your ground, and after you have done everything, to stand. Stand firm."*

16

Cobra Capture

....

*"Fear and trembling seized me and made all
my bones shake."* **Job 4:14**

*"Yea, though I walk through the valley of the shadow of death, I
will fear no evil; For You are with me; Your rod and Your staff,
they comfort me."* **Psalm 23:4 (NKJV)**

In our ministry in Africa, survival in our village often depended on missionaries and local people sharing their skills with each other. I was certainly not a snake handler. While snakes are interesting creatures and have their place in the environment, I just don't like them. It was always good for me to be able to call on those who would catch venomous snakes.

The village of Maun where we lived and worked for seven years was blessed with a couple of brave men, Henry and William, who had established a business of processing deadly snake venom. Mary and I had become friends with them and would visit their facility as they milked cobras, black mambas, and other species of deadly snakes to obtain their venom. It was certainly an educational experience. On the other hand, it was a little unnerving to be standing in a room with someone who had a dangerous snake wrapped around his arm as his hand held it firmly just behind the head. We had to have confidence in the skills of these men, that they would not drop or lose control of the viper. We developed a lot of respect for their vital skills and their contribution to the medical field, resulting in the saving of hundreds of lives.

Henry and William kept many deadly venomous snakes in their facility, and they had to maintain the health of the snakes by providing food and care. They would limit collecting the snake venom to once a week per snake so as to not stress them. To milk a snake, the men would use a small glass beaker with a thin, plastic film stretched across the top. With the snake firmly secure, the handler would squeeze its jaws, opening the mouth. The fangs would drop down, and the handler would press the back of the viper's head, pushing the fangs through the thin plastic on top of the beaker. At this time, the handler would carefully press the sides of the head, forcing the venom into the beaker. Once complete, the snake was carefully placed back in its cage and fed.

The venom had a great monetary value. It would carefully be removed from the beaker, placed on a glass slide, and then put in a bell jar, where a vacuum pump would remove the air. In time the venom would dry, turning to a crystal residue on the glass. The crystallized venom would be scraped off, weighed, and placed in secure containers. It was then shipped to pharmaceutical companies to process, producing serum for antivenom snakebite kits. The serum would then become a lifesaver for the many snakebite victims every year. It was a very profitable business for the men of the village, netting them hundreds or thousands of dollars per gram for the dried, crystalized venom.

It was for this reason that my friends who milked the snakes asked me to contact them whenever a deadly venomous snake was on the mission grounds. I called them often. They removed several deadly snakes from the property. Killing the snakes was always my last resort.

One evening I spotted the tracks of a cobra at the entrance of the mission facility. The tracks led to a bush near the mission house. Knowing the snake was in the bush, I alerted my family to remain inside. I walked the short distance where the snake handlers had their business. Only one of the men was present. The other was away on a trip. The fellow said he would come and get the cobra. He picked up a burlap bag, and we walked back to the mission house in the dark.

I had my flashlight with me, so we checked the tracks, confirming the cobra had not left the area. We found the five-foot creature still in the bush. It was attracted to the light. Its forked tongue was sensing everything around it. Henry and his partner usually worked as a team catching the snakes, but he was alone this time. I wasn't sure how he planned to handle the problem, so I waited for his next move.

Without warning, Henry turned to me and said, "Are you ready? Here is what I want you to do. Remain facing the cobra. Stand to the side with your arm straight out, and shine the light on the head of the snake. If it tries to strike, you will be able to jerk your arm back, and it will miss you.

"I will go around to the back of the bush and locate its tail," he continued. "With a firm grasp, I will get it by the tail and drag it out."

I wasn't too fond of being the target in this "catch a cobra" game, but I did want to have the deadly snake removed from the grounds. Standing out of the direct strike path, I continued flashing the beam of light on the snake's head. It moved back and forth and tried to position itself for a strike. I was prepared to jerk my arm back if were to strike; however, I had no backup plan should it suddenly jump out and land on the ground near me in the dark.

"I've got it! Get the burlap bag," Henry yelled. He grasped its tail and pulled. I saw the head of the snake disappear from the light. I wasn't sure just what I was getting myself into at this point, but having found myself now part of the cobra-catching team, I had to act quickly.

"Open the bag wide and hold it tight," Henry said as he held up the cobra by its tail. It was swinging back and forth, attempting to pull itself up and over his arm, and he kept jerking his arm shaking it down. In the moonlight, I held the burlap bag open as Henry approached me, holding the deadly cobra as it swung back and forth, frightened and ready to strike anything in its path. My forehead was covered with beads of perspiration. Adrenalin rushed through my body. My heart was racing.

The plan was for him to lower the venomous snake into the opening of the burlap bag head first, between swings. As he slowly lowered the snake, it attempted to strike anything near. When its head was just a few inches above my hands, Henry said he was ready to drop the snake in the bag. He told me to hold the burlap bag firmly and be ready to close the top of the bag.

Faith Journeys

With a thump, the cobra hit the bottom of the bag. I quickly secured the top, and Henry took the bag. Our mission was accomplished. I was rid of the snake, and he had another snake to add to his collection. Once again the mission grounds had been cleared of a danger. It happened as a result of teamwork.

Our journey of faith often involves faith in those with whom we work. Building relationships and trust allows us to network and achieve much in our effort to help others. My faith in Henry's snake-catching skills, and his faith in my ability to assist him, resulted in a successful outcome.

In the Old Testament we read, *"Though one may be overpowered, two can defend themselves. A cord of three strands is not quickly broken."* (Ecclesiastes 4:12) This verse says people are better together, that God's plan is for us to work together. We live in a world filled with evil and injustice, but in Christ, we have each other.

We are interdependent on each other, and so it is important that we interact and work together in our families, churches, communities, nation, and world. Faith and trust develop event by event, experience by experience, like steps in a journey. We do not walk that journey alone.

17

Double Danger

"Let my persecutors be put to shame, but keep me from shame; let them be terrified, but keep me from terror. Bring on them the day of disaster; destroy them with double destruction." **Jeremiah 17:18**

In life the unexpected is always just around the corner. When everything appears normal, problems can emerge without warning. For this reason, it is important to remember where we have been, how God has led us and rescued us in the past, and where our present choices may take us. Our faith must remain strong.

When we were living in Maun, Botswana, Mary and I kept a large box for wood in the corner by the back door of the mission house. One day we learned in a dramatic way that it was the perfect hiding place for one of Africa's most dangerous creatures.

The mission was a very busy place. Mission workers and pastors were on the grounds all day. In addition to Mary and me and our two children, two African children were living in the mission house with us as well as an orphan teen. Snakes crisscrossed the grounds on a regular basis. Some of Africa's most deadly poisonous snakes would come and go on the property all the time. It was possible that snakes might be at our feet or over our heads in a tree at any time, day or night. It was important that

Faith Journeys

we keep the venomous snake population under control to protect the children and others.

It was late one night when our dogs began barking. Wildlife often came around, so I knew something had entered the perimeter of the mission grounds. In the African remote backcountry, Mary and I never knew what creatures we might encounter in the dark of the night. We had learned to move with caution among foliage, especially after dark, for many snakes were on the move.

I got my flashlight and exited the back door. The dogs would direct me to the intruder. They were barking and pawing at the wood box by the back door. I checked the sandy ground, and in the beam of my flashlight I saw snake tracks leading behind the box.

I could not leave a deadly snake hiding behind the wood box. The children would be out to play in the morning. Mary and I would be getting wood from the box to put in the kitchen stove. I had fought snakes with sticks and stones before; however, the most effective weapon for use against a snake is a shotgun. The dogs would keep the snake cornered until I returned with my shotgun.

On my return, I carefully approached one end of the large box, which was only a few inches from the wall of the house. The other end of the box was against the house, so the snake had only one way in and out. I told the dogs to stand down while I dealt with the snake.

As I shined my flashlight in the opening, I could see a cobra. I held the shotgun tight against my hip, keeping my other hand on my light where it was focused to ensure the cobra did not attempt to strike me. I squeezed the trigger, and a blast of buckshot filled the space between the wood box and the wall of the house where the cobra was located.

I felt reasonably secure there was little chance I had missed the snake. As the smoke from the gun blast cleared, I saw the remains of the snake, its head missing. I got a yard rake and pulled the wood box back a bit so I could drag the body of the snake out. It was about five foot long. I then shined the light around, looking for the head. Since the head contains the venom, I felt it necessary to locate it.

I saw what I thought was the snake's head. The mouth was slowly opening and closing. I thought it was just a muscle reaction of the dying part of the snake. I took my rake and hooked it on the head to remove it, only to find a heavy resistance. It quickly became apparent that I was

80

dragging a second dying cobra out that just happened to catch the over-spray of my shotgun blast.

One shot fired in the dark resulted in two dead cobras and one fortunate missionary protected by the Lord. I could have missed the second cobra. I could have reached my hand in to pull the first dead cobra out, only to be bitten by the second one. It was God who had called and sent us to live among the vipers, and he alone was our Protector.

The devil in the Scripture is not only compared to a roaring lion seeking to devour us, but also to a cunning, deceptive serpent, often hard to see until it is too late. The devil is deceitful, setting snares and traps in an attempt to destroy our relationship with God. In the garden of Eden, Adam and Eve wrestled between choices of right and wrong, good and evil. Sadly, they were snared by the serpent. Because of their example, we can be the wiser.

Often one temptation is only a setup for something worse in life. Two snakes may be lying in wait when we think we are facing only one. Jeremiah was right when he said, *"Destroy them with double destruction."* (Jeremiah 17:18)

Many people of Jeremiah's day had abandoned their faith and become critical and bitter. Our faith must remain strong, and we must not doubt and have bitterness as they did. And we must live a life of spiritual awareness in order to avoid the many temptations. The disciple James said, *"Each person is tempted when they are dragged away by their own evil desire and enticed."* (James 1:14)

We can be victorious. *"No temptation has overtaken you except what is common to mankind. And God is faithful; he will not let you be tempted beyond what you can bear. But when you are tempted, he will also provide a way out so that you can endure it."* (1 Corinthians 10:13)

18

Almost Blinded

"I have been constantly on the move. I have been in danger." **2 Corinthians 11:26**

"Like the blind we grope along the wall, feeling our way like people without eyes. At midday we stumble as if it were twilight; among the strong, we are like the dead." **Isaiah 59:10**

Spiritual blindness can be as disabling as physical blindness. Without faith, we grope in darkness, stumbling to find our way. All of us encounter the risk of spiritual blindness by Satan, the proverbial serpent, but once I had an encounter with a deadly snake that can cause physical blindness.

Our mission grounds in Maun, Botswana, were adjacent to a heavy jungle brush area near the Thamalakane River. The entire grounds had a fence around them with a front gate to provide protection from wildlife. By the gate, just inside, was a small tree. One night as I was returning home after a day in Xgaraxlau, I was greeted by an unwelcome guest.

It was already dark, and the moon was full. As I passed under the tree, I heard a rustling in the leaves. Glancing over my shoulder, I saw movement in the tree above my head. Most likely another of the many snakes had entered the mission compound. I went into the house, picked up my flashlight, and went back out to check the tree.

The men in the village who captured venomous snakes, collected the venom, and sold it to pharmaceutical companies to produce antivenom snakebite kits were well aware of the large number of snakes in and around the mission property, and I had already agreed to contact them whenever it was feasible. But if they were not available, I had told them, I would have to eliminate the venomous vipers on my own.

Since it was already well past dark, and knowing the men were out on one of the delta islands hunting, I assessed what action to take. My first objective was to determine what kind of snake it was. Cautiously I shined the light into the tree.

It is not uncommon for snakes to climb trees. Several venomous snakes in Africa do. The *boomslang*, or tree snake, is one of many that climb trees. Each snake's venom varies in how it affects humans. The boomslang can deliver deadly, hemotoxic venom.

Other snakes, including those in the cobra family, are often found in trees. The second most dangerous venomous snake in Africa is the spitting cobra, one commonly feared by the people. While the bite of the snake can be deadly, the snake also has the unique ability to project its venom through the air, targeting the eyes of its victim. Furthermore, it can do so with great accuracy up to several feet away. When the venom hits the eyes, it immediately causes extreme pain and can result in permanent blindness. With the victim disabled, the snake can escape or strike again if necessary.

As I searched the tree with my light, I suddenly saw my greatest fear, the dreaded spitting cobra. The snake was located overhead and slightly to my right. It was firmly wrapped around a limb, and it had swung its head back with its mouth wide open. The projection fangs were visible. What happened in the next seconds seemed to play out in slow motion.

With sling shot action, it struck. In a split second, visible in the beam of my light, I saw the venom spray coming down like rain. I knew I was only a fraction of a second from being hit. There was no escape. My body responded instantly in defensive action, but not before God permitted a quick visual transmission to the brain of the trajectory of the airborne venom.

I closed both eyes tightly and ducked my head. I felt the lethal venom splatter over my face. Immediately I tilted my head face down to allow the venom to drip off. I had to keep it from running down my forehead, if possible.

I stumbled away from the tree in the dark with my head still face down. Staggering along through the dark, not knowing where the cobra had gone, I made it to the side of the mission house. I followed the wall of the house by feel to the door and called out to Mary, keeping my eyes tightly closed and face down.

Mary heard me calling and rushed out to find out what had happened. I quickly explained to her that my face had been splattered with cobra venom. Part of our survival training involved such emergencies, so she knew what to do. She knew it had to be thoroughly flushed away and cleaned, so she took immediate action, bringing me soap and a towel.

After thoroughly washing my face with soap and flushing it with water, I carefully dried it with a towel. There could be no remaining water on my face that could get in my eyes because of possible traces of venom residue. Also, I knew any portion of the powerful snake venom that might remain in the towel could dry, only to be reactivated again if the towel were to be used. Because of the risk, the towel would have to be burned.

With my head still down, I carefully opened my eyes. The lanterns inside the house were burning, giving a soft glow of light, but even with the soft glow of the lanterns, I felt like a deer in the headlights of a car. Ever so carefully, I opened and closed my eyes, testing to see if there was any effect from the snake strike. When I was sure there was none, I thanked God, giving him credit for my quick reactions and for preventing possible permanent blindness or death.

The danger was yet not over. I still had a deadly snake on the property and the responsibility to keep my family safe. I would have to determine where the snake was and kill it. The venom residue under the tree and any other residue that had dripped from my face along my path to the house would also have to be dealt with as well.

I made my way back in the darkness of the night to find my flashlight. In the moonlight, I found it lying on the ground. Picking it up, I carefully checked out the tree again. I kept my arm outstretched to my side, holding the light, so if the snake were to attempt another attack, it would aim for the light and not my face.

The snake was no longer in the tree. My concern then became where it had gone. I picked up its track at the base of the tree, leading away through the fence and into the brush behind the house. For the time being, it was gone. The next day I would need to look for any spots of dried venom in the sand and dispose of them. It was time for a good night's rest and another thankful praise to God for his continual protection.

The Bible states that God is not willing that any person should perish. While God is not willing that any person should perish, Satan, the old serpent, seeks our destruction. We are continually bombarded with venomous ideas and choices in an effort to blind us spiritually. Our eternal destiny depends on our choices.

We may feel that life is all about us, our personal pleasure, and our comfort. In reality, we are spiritual beings, housed in earthly bodies, with eternity-bound souls. It is for this reason our Creator has made provisions to protect our spiritual eyesight. *"I will lead the blind by ways they have not known, along unfamiliar paths I will guide them; I will turn the darkness into light before them and make the rough places smooth. These are the things I will do; I will not forsake them."* (Isaiah 42:16) *"The LORD gives sight to the blind, the LORD lifts up those who are bowed down, the LORD loves the righteous."* (Psalm 146:8)

19

Black Mamba

"Anyone who trembles with fear may turn back and leave." **Judges 7:3**

None of us escape times of fear in our journey through life. Missionaries in the remote areas of Africa and other parts of the world frequently encounter danger. Threats can come from both physical and spiritual places. If there were a list of snakes that could best be compared to the evil force of Satan, I would place the *black mamba* high on that list. The black mamba can move faster than we can, up to twelve miles an hour. It has an aggressive attitude and can bite repeatedly, each bite enough to kill. Without immediate action, the one bitten will die.

Most snakes move about at night, and this is true of the dreaded black mamba, a venomous snake listed in the top ten of the most dangerous in the world. It is the most deadly and dangerous snake on the African continent. I am fortunate to be alive today, having survived a late night, surprise attack by a black mamba. God's protective hand was present to deliver me.

My family and I lived a simple life, day by day, in faith that God would supply our needs. Oftentimes the local people would share food with us. It was important for us to economize as much as possible, keeping our personal budget low, so that much of the funds sent to us from people in

Faith Journeys

the USA would be available for the work of the mission. To minimize our living expenses, we raised as much of our own food as possible.

At the mission, we had a simple wood-framed hen house and a fenced-in chicken yard with a gate. We raised chickens to provided meat and eggs. We also had guinea fowls, which made an excellent security system with their loud shrieking sounds when disturbed. Often at night, jackals and other similar creatures would come around and attack our chickens. We were always on our guard to protect both the chickens and ourselves.

It was late one night when we heard a loud racket coming from the chicken yard. The guinea fowls were shrieking, and the chickens were agitated by their loud noise. The only weapon I had available at the time was an old, British-made, Wesley Richards 318 single shot rifle. It had the power to stop a lion attack or turn a charging elephant, if needed; however, it was a single shot and overpowered for dealing with snakes. Regardless, since it was the only gun available at the time, I took my gun and my flashlight and headed for the hen house. I expected to encounter another jackal.

Most of the chickens and guinea fowl were out of the hen house and in the chicken yard, running and squawking, while a few others were still inside in the chicken coop in a state of panic. It was apparent that the perpetrator was inside the hen house. As a precaution, I first looked for any snake tracks in the sand. Snakes were always around where we lived, and it had become necessary for me to learn how to track them.

Each snake makes a unique pattern in the dirt. You can tell, by looking at the tracks, which direction the snake is moving and what kind of snake it probably is. You can also get a good idea about what size the snake is.

The chances of locating any tracks in the sandy chicken yard had been greatly diminished by the squawking guinea fowl and agitated chickens. In their excitement and running around, they had greatly disturbed the soil all over the chicken yard. I was still of the opinion that the most likely culprit was a jackal, since snakes generally don't attack chickens— unless it was a python looking for a snack. Other snakes would go after baby chicks or steal eggs.

I carefully opened the gate to the chicken yard and walked in, prepared to confront the perpetrator. I felt reasonably secure, prepared, and in control of the situation. What was about to happen, however, was far from my imagination, and I was totally unprepared. Little did I know I was facing a battle of survival for my life. Looking back, I see I could have died that night in the chicken yard.

Still thinking a jackal had crawled under the fence, I stopped at the door of the hen house. The chickens inside were still squawking in a state of panic, confirming something was greatly disturbing them. I braced myself for action, pointed my rifle at the door, and kicked it open.

Without warning a deadly black mamba raced directly toward me. I was staring certain death in the face unless somehow I stopped the attack. I had no black mamba antivenom available, and I knew a bite would be fatal. Without quick action and divine intervention, I would be totally at the mercy of the attacking, deadly snake.

In a split second, I took aim in the dark at the fast-moving target and fired. I missed. The deadly snake, raised off the ground, raced directly at me. Before I could move, it began to coil around the end of my gun barrel, heading straight for my face. Its mouth was wide open, ready for a strike.

My God-given senses kicked in, and I jerked the rifle upward, lifting the snake off the ground and breaking its ability to continue up the gun barrel. As soon as I broke the momentum of the fast-moving snake, I swung the gun in a downward motion, slinging the black mamba off my gun barrel to the ground.

There was no time to reload the gun, so in military fashion, I did a quick whirl of the gun, reversing my hands holding the gun barrel instead of the stock. I needed the broad base and weight of the gunstock to continue the fight. All of these motions happened in just a few seconds and a whirl of activity. There was no time to think the matter through. I was fighting for my life, and my reactions were totally on God-given autopilot.

After I broke the advance movement of the black mamba and slung it off my gun barrel to the ground, it prepared for another attack. This time it struck directly at me. In response, I swung the gun like a baseball bat, striking the snake in mid-air. Slightly stunned, it prepared to strike again as I jumped back, dancing with fear and knowing it was certain death if it bit me. I kept focused on its every move.

Sure enough, it struck again, and a second swing of my gunstock gave it another hard blow. The snake, more stunned than before, attempted to coil to prepare for yet another strike. At this point I began pounding the head of the black mamba with the stock of the gun. I hit it so violently, over and over, blow after blow, that I cracked my gunstock.

The snake was subdued, at least for the moment, and it was certainly time for my retreat. I had temporarily won the battle, but the war was not over. I carefully backed away in an adrenaline rush that had my heart pounding out of my chest.

I returned to the mission house and picked up more shells and a brighter light. Fully prepared this time, I cautiously returned to the chicken yard. The hens and guinea fowl had quieted down. When I arrived, the black mamba was gone.

I followed the snake's tracks out of the chicken yard. They led into the heavy brush behind the mission compound. I continued tracking it in the bush for a while to ensure it had left the area. No sign of it. The war was over, and a shaken guy with a cracked gunstock from the fight of his life returned to the mission house to get some rest for the night. By the grace of God, my Creator, I survived that night of terror.

The Psalmist expressed the feeling I had that night well. *"Yea, though I walk through the valley of the shadow of death, I will fear no evil: for thou art with me; thy rod and thy staff they comfort me"* (Psalm 23:4 KJV).

When serving God, missionaries who work in difficult areas of the world often must put their lives in danger. Even more, thousands of Christians for centuries have been martyred around the world. Many suffer terrible experiences, even as Christ himself did on the cross. They are imprisoned and sometimes tortured for following Christ.

God has promised that even in the valley of the shadow of death, he will be with his people. He was certainly with me the night I fought off the black mamba attack. That experience, while terrifying from the human point of view, was another of testing of my faith. It reinforced my dependence on God, teaching me once again to place my continual trust in God.

20

A Cobra Comes to Church

"On this rock I will build my church, and the gates of Hades will not overcome it." **Matthew 16:18**

Life was simple in the village. None of us had electricity or running water. Phones were nonexistent, and all of us got our water from the river. The people of the village loved to come to the mission to study the Word of God. Anyone who cared to know could always tell the number of people attending service by counting the walking sticks, which were left by the front door during services. Everyone carried a walking stick in those days to have an immediate means of defense against the many poisonous snakes that roamed the area.

Our first African church building in Maun, Botswana, was very primitive in its construction. We cut forked poles from the woods to use for wall support posts. The poles were stripped of the bark, which was then used to tie the horizontal wall poles to the forked wall support posts. A rafter support system was made of hand cut trees to hold the grass roof. The walls were made of reeds gathered from the river. A floor made of a mixture of cow dung and termite mound dirt completed our little place of worship. This primitive building would later be replaced by a building of handmade bricks, built on the same location.

Faith Journeys

This simple building had replaced our brush arbor gathering location, where we first had begun holding worship services under a tree some time before. The logs we had used for pews in the brush arbor were moved to the church building for seating. During services or Bible studies, the men would sit on the logs placed on one side of the room, and the women would sit on the logs on the other side. Such was the way we worshiped in the Kubung District of the village of Maun.

Everyone coming to the service that Sunday morning had gathered at the church for the Sunday morning Bible study. We were rapidly outgrowing our thatch-reed facility, so we had added a reed grass roof room to the main building. Mary had the children outside under a tree for their gathering. The young people were in the main sanctuary. I had the senior adult class in the added room on the church.

The grass-roofed, reed-walled addition provided shade from the sun and shelter from the rain. However, it was easily accessible to the numerous wild creatures that inhabited the area. The broom we used to sweep was kept in the room where I was teaching that morning.

The room was packed with men and women gathered around me, sitting on the floor. I was about halfway through my lesson when I saw a cobra slithering in through the doorway. Others saw it too, and there was instant pandemonium. Everyone jumped up and raced out the doorway as the cobra continued in. I could hear the women chanting, "Yah, yah, yah, yah, yah," as they fled the place.

The only thing I had to defend myself with was the broom in the corner of the room, so I grabbed it and prepared for the attack. By then the cobra and I were the only ones left in the room.

The cobra raced across the room into a corner. I quickly took the broom and shoved it against the snake, pressing hard against it and the reed wall. The cobra was pinned down, extremely angry, and ready to strike. I pressed even harder as it attempted to wiggle free. Its head and front part of its body weaved back and forth, trying to strike me. I feared it would free itself anytime, and I certainly could not turn it loose and run. A broom was not the weapon of choice to fight off a cobra.

I heard a commotion outside, and suddenly about a half dozen brave Christian women came rushing back into the classroom, carrying their snake sticks. Without hesitation, they attacked the cobra as I held it down. The clicking and thumping sound of the sticks pounding the

A Cobra Comes to Church

cobra was almost musical. As they beat the cobra and chanted at the same time, I felt sorry for the critter. It did not have a chance against the fury of these African ladies.

The men looked through the door, watching the battle take place. I was surprised to see them and considered joining them. Apparently these ladies had done this before.

With the cobra no longer a threat to anyone, I tossed it out of our classroom and resumed our Bible studies. The incident had no impact on our attendance. The following Sunday, the facility was packed again for another service.

Jesus said, *"On this rock I will build my church, and the gates of Hades will not overcome it"* (Matthew 16:18). When followers of Christ gather, the old serpent Satan desires to disrupt and destroy. Relationships, however, are part of the plan of God. Our relationship to God is vital for our spiritual awareness and deliverance. Our relationship with one another is vital for our spiritual growth and builds faith.

The devil will focus on our emotional feelings and desire for self-preservation. He will attempt to drive us into destructive behaviors that can damage or destroy relationships with others. Just as the cobra totally disrupted our Bible study at the mission, so the devil attacks and tries to destroy congregations. The unified effort of the African women destroyed the cobra. The Christ-centered, unified spirit of believers can dispose of the evil force of the old serpent, the devil, that seeks to disrupt and destroy.

21

The Cobra and the Mother Hen

"Jerusalem, Jerusalem, you who kill the prophets and stone those sent to you, how often I have longed to gather your children together, as a hen gathers her chicks under her wings, and you were not willing." **Matthew 23:37**

Almost every family in our village in Maun, Botswana, had chickens. In any direction you would go, you would see a mother hen with her chicks, scratching the dirt as the chicks were feeding. Jesus once talked about the commitment that a mother hen has for her chicks. He pointed out that in his love and concern for the spiritual welfare of people, he is like a mother hen that gathers her chicks under her wings. He cares for those he loves. One day the truth of Jesus' words became real in my life.

Mary and my's mother hen with chicks would often roam free on the mission grounds during the day. Because many snakes moved about at night, we had a perimeter of sand around the mission house that we would brush down every evening with a large branch. In the morning, we would check the perimeter to see if there were any fresh snake tracks. If so, I would track the snake down and deal with it.

I was always up early before sunrise to prepare for the new day. As soon as it was light, I would check the grounds for any snakes that might have entered the area. As I walked into the yard behind the house one morning, I saw a mother hen dead, lying in the yard. She had baby chicks scampering around her.

As I examined the area, I saw where a battle between the mother hen and a snake had taken place. Chicken tracks and cobra tracks were all over the area. Feathers were scattered on the ground. On closer examination, I saw the fatal bite of the cobra on the neck of the mother hen. The cobra had come for her chicks, and she had gone into battle in an effort to save them. She did all she could and died in the process.

God is not willing that any should perish. For this reason, Jesus died on the cross that we might live. *"For God so loved the world that he gave his one and only Son, that whoever believes in him shall not perish but have eternal life"* (John 3:16). *"Very truly I tell you, unless a kernel of wheat falls to the ground and dies, it remains only a single seed. But if it dies, it produces many seeds"* (John 12:24). *"Therefore, I urge you, brothers and sisters, in view of God's mercy, to offer your bodies as a living sacrifice, holy and pleasing to God—this is your true and proper worship"* (Romans 12:1).

The mother hen sacrificed her life for her chicks. Christ sacrificed his life for you and me. A living sacrifice requires faith. In our faith journey, there are times when getting *out of the box* is necessary. There is more to life than living in our comfort zone. Faith is necessary when we give our lives, our time, our concern, and our compassion in service, helping those less fortunate.

22

The Black Mamba in the Living Room

"For he guards the course of the just and protects the way of his faithful ones." **Proverbs 2:8**

I often had to be away from the mission house in Botswana during the day to work on the many projects for the mission. In addition to managing the main site, I was responsible to work with the local pastors, who were planting congregations in other villages throughout the area. We had several places of worship under construction, where the people were making bricks and cutting wood used for cooking. Adult literacy classes were taking place in other villages as well. Each day I would travel to the different sites to check with all the mission workers to see what their needs were.

The mission was a very busy place. Mary was teaching sewing, cooking, and knitting classes. We had two small orphan African children, David and Bambi, living with us in addition to our two children, and Gloria, an orphan teen. Mary and Gloria would care for the younger children.

During this time, we were able to rent a house from the British government. It was a nice facility with a fenced-in yard. We had a wood-burning stove in the kitchen to cook on. Using wood to burn over time resulted in the walls becoming smoked, so they would have to be cleaned and repainted from time to time.

Faith Journeys

We always had occasional critters that would come and go, such as jackals, monkeys, and other small animals. Scorpions too would get in the house from time to time. We even found one in the baby bed one day. It was at this house where I was stung on the bottom of my foot when a scorpion crawled under my sandal as I was walking. Many cobras and other snakes including the black mamba would frequent the property as well.

This was the setting where a black mamba chose to enter our house one day. I often wondered if it was the one I had fought with in the chicken yard that escaped into the brush behind our house. I was away at the time, and Mary was at home working on projects in the living room. On this day, the government had sent a crew of workers to paint the smoked walls of the kitchen. The men had set up a scaffold in the doorway between the kitchen and living room. Our baby daughter, Sally, was sitting under the scaffold on the floor in the kitchen doorway.

From where Mary was working in the living room, she could see the back kitchen door. It was in direct line with the entryway into the living room where Sally was sitting. The workers had been coming and going out the kitchen door, so they had propped open the back door while they worked.

Suddenly Mary saw a black mamba slither in the kitchen door, heading straight for our little girl. She knew that a child would grab at something such as the snake if it crawled over her legs as she sat on the floor. Mary knew our daughter would not have a chance if the black mamba were to bite her. She instantly called out to the Lord in a prayer, "Lord, protect my baby." The Word of God says, *"For he guards the course of the just and protects the way of his faithful ones."* (Proverbs 2:8)

In the seconds the black mamba entered the back door into the kitchen and Mary called on the Lord for help, she saw a hand reach down and grab our little girl by the arm, lifting her to safety as the black mamba slithered underneath her. God had heard Mary's prayer. Seconds from our daughter being bitten by a deadly venomous snake, she had been rescued by the man on the scaffold. God had provided a way of escape, protecting our little girl.

The snake then came into the living room where Mary was working. Another worker, aware the black mamba had entered the house, rushed in with a club and stones. With baby Sally safely on the scaffold, secured by one worker, Mary and the other worker chased the venomous snake into the corner of the room, where they were able to stone and beat it to death.

Certainly God was with our family that day. What ended up with the removal of a dead black mamba from our living room could have been a tragic day at the mission had it not been for the hand of God and the hand of an alert painter on a scaffold. God protected Mary and the worker, who risked their lives to destroy the intruder.

And just as the strong hand of the African worker on the scaffold saved a child, so the hand of God is always poised, ready to reach down and lift us out of the dangerous circumstances we encounter. *"The LORD gives sight to the blind, the LORD lifts up those who are bowed down, the LORD loves the righteous."* (Psalm 146:8)

Part III

The Caribbean, Latin
America, and Later Years

23

Village Lanterns

"You, LORD, keep my lamp burning; my God turns my darkness into light." **Psalm 18:28**

I was eighteen years old and a freshman in college when I made my first trip outside the USA. The Spanish class I was in decided to go to Mexico for a volunteer work camp. Our trip was over spring break and was a volunteer opportunity for cultural exchange and to enhance our learning of the Spanish language.

I had already been involved in sharing the gospel in migrant work camps in the USA in my early teens, so I was very interested in visiting the people of Mexico and learning more about their country as well as learning about a new culture. I remembered the words from a song, "This little light of mine, I'm going to let it shine," that I had sung as a child, so I wanted to be able to witness and share God's love with others. This trip was my first opportunity to let my light shine outside the borders of my homeland. It was also a time when I learned about the importance of sharing the light of the gospel from newfound friends in a country other than mine.

The Spanish professor, affectionately called "Pop DeShayes," led the team of ten students. He had a great heart for missions and often traveled to the Church of God mission, La Buena Tierra, in Saltillo, Mexico, which was our destination for this trip. All of the students loved him,

Faith Journeys

and he was a great influence on our lives. He would become one of many who contributed to the shaping and molding of my faith.

We packed and loaded into cars for the drive from Houston, Texas, to the mission in Saltillo, located in the mountains of central Mexico. When we arrived, I saw what I had read about in books unfolding before my eyes. Even with my preparation, the reality of the poverty I encountered ripped at my heart and brought tears to my eyes. I thought of the poor migrant workers I had seen in the USA having to live in old rail boxcars. I could not understand why they were not provided better living arrangements, and here in Mexico I was seeing another kind of deep poverty.

After settling in at the mission, we traveled higher into the mountains to a small rural village that was spread out over the hillside. The people of the area lived in extreme poverty by American standards. There was no electricity, running water, or other utilities available. The homes were small, simple, adobe mud brick structures to provide protection from the elements. The people shared a community well. Compassion brought tearing to our eyes as our small group experienced their extreme poverty as compared to our standard of living back home. God was using professor De Shayes, who brought us here, to help shape our hearts and prepare us for a life of service to God and others.

A Christian family living in the mountains had invited us to their home for the evening meal before the service at a nearby church. When we arrived, the mother of the family was busy preparing refried beans and handmade tortillas cooked on a wood-burning stove. Wood smoke drifted throughout the house as bright-eyed children with big smiles watched our every move. Visitors did not often stop by their home.

The sun was beginning to set, so the father checked the oil in the lantern and lit it so there would be light in the house. We finished our meal and had a wonderful time visiting with the family. They had made us feel very welcome. In the distance we could see the church silhouetted in the sunset. Soon darkness blanketed the landscape.

As we were ready to leave for service, the father took the family lantern and led the way to the church. He had the keys and went early to unlock. We walked along with him and his family as he led the way.

We arrived and entered the building. His lantern gave off a soft, orange glow in the church. At first the light was very dim. As our eyes adjusted, in the shadows we saw long wooden shelves that ran along both sides of the building. I expected the father to place his lantern next to us where his family and our group were seated. Instead he took the lantern and placed it on one of shelves along the wall and then returned to sit with his family.

At the entrance of the church, I could see the beautiful, starlit sky. Out over the countryside, I could see small lights seemingly dancing as they bobbed along. It soon was apparent that each light moving toward the church represented another family with a lantern, arriving for the service.

As each family came into the church, a family member quietly took the family lantern and placed it on one of the shelves along the sides of the building. In a matter of minutes, the church was filled with people and lanterns they had placed on the long shelves along the walls. The whole inside of the church building had a soft glow with enough light for everyone.

A powerful message became apparent from the event that had unfolded before me. Jesus explained that we are the light of the world and that we should not hide the light or keep it to ourselves. We should set our light on a stand where all could see it. These people literally had demonstrated the words of Jesus by what they had done. They unselfishly shared their light for the benefit of all.

As the service began, our hands were free to praise the Lord, and we all had adequate light to see. A father and his lamp had taught me a lesson about unity, sharing, and caring for others. The actions of the Christian families, sharing their lamps in the mountains of Mexico, reinforced my understanding of the power of unity and of letting one's light shine. This experience was another stone added to the foundation of my faith.

As Christians we have so much to share, so much light to shine from our lives. We must join together and raise our lanterns high so that others see the radiance of God's love and unity. Our living example of Christ within us can give a continual, warm glow to all around us. *"How good and pleasant it is when God's people live together in unity."* (Psalm 133:1) *"And over all these virtues put on love, which binds them all together in perfect unity."* (Colossians 3:14)

Fifty years later, I had the privilege to return to Saltillo, Mexico, and visit with those who were children at the time of my first visit. The spiritual light of the mountain village was still shining in the lives of the next generation.

24

The Rental

....

"It will be a shelter and shade from the heat of the day, and a refuge and hiding place from the storm and rain." **Isaiah 4:6**

In 1970, with the ministry in Botswana well established and local leadership in place, God called us to relocate in Latin America. We pastored a small church in Puerto Rico for a couple of years. Our third daughter, Rachel, was born in San Juan. Over the years, our journey of faith had led us high in the mountains of Tanzania and across the Kalahari Desert. We now found ourselves on an island, once again looking to God for his provision.

When we first arrived, we rented a small house on a very small lot. It had limited space for what we needed, and it was located on the opposite side of the city where we were planning to work. It was temporary accommodations. When we learned that the owner would be returning to reclaim the house, we knew we would have to move by the end of the month. We started looking for a new mission house. In yet another step in our journey of faith, we waited on the Lord to intervene and provide.

Our desire was to find a property in the area where we were working in San Juan. After checking several possible locations, we found what we felt would be perfect. It was a nice facility with additional buildings on the property. It was about two acres, and the entire property was walled

Faith Journeys

in with a gate at the drive. The property also had banana trees, a coffee tree, and orange, grapefruit, lemon, and other fruit trees. There were also coconut palms on the property. It would be an excellent place for a mission base. We felt that God had led us to this location and that we would be able to carry out our ministry there.

Information for the property was listed on the rental sign posted on the gate, and it gave the address of the owner. I was excited to have found the place, and in my mind, I had already begun planning how we could develop it into a functional mission base. I took down the address and made my way there.

I remembered the apostle Paul had written, *"God will meet all your needs according to the riches of his glory in Christ Jesus"* (Philippians 4:19). Also, in the book of Isaiah is written, *"It will be a shelter and shade from the heat of the day, and a refuge and hiding place from the storm and rain"* (Isaiah 4:6). We certainly had a *need* for a *shelter*, I thought.

I went to the door of the owner and told him we were interested in renting the property. He looked at me and said, "Oh, I am sorry. I forgot to take the sign down. Someone has already placed a deposit on the property and will be moving in next weekend." He apologized again, and I walked back to the car and left. Time was running out on finding a place, so I knew I would have to keep looking.

This scenario was not the first time we had encountered an obstacle in meeting a need. Several years earlier while in Africa, we really needed a transport truck. We located one, but in that case, we did not have the funds to purchase it. We prayed that if God wanted to provide the truck for the mission, it would still be there when we came back for supplies in a couple months. On our return, the truck was still there. The dealer selling it had reduced the price because it had not sold. Everyone who had looked at it ended up choosing another vehicle, he said. We knew then that God had reserved the transport truck for the mission, so we bought it.

Could it possibly be that God could still provide us with the rental property I had looked at in San Juan? I certainly felt God had led us to the location. I drove about a block away and felt I needed to park the car and pray. My prayer was simple, as most were. "Lord, I felt you led us to that property, but it has been rented. What should I do next?" As strange as it seemed, I felt I should return to the man who had told me the property had been rented.

The Rental

I had spent a lifetime trying to maintain a balance between facts and feelings. Once again my faith would be put to a test. I wrestled with the idea of returning to the home of the owner of the rental. I could risk embarrassing myself. Or I could return in faith that God was intervening. At the worst, the man would only laugh, and I would be embarrassed and leave.

It had been about a half an hour since I left the owner's house. It is hard to explain, but the feeling to return was so strong that I felt I had to follow my feelings. I tried to be realistic about the matter, but I knew there are unique times in life that believers must step out in faith. I wondered what I would say to the man.

I drove up in front of the house and got out of the car. I did not rush to the door. Many thoughts were going through my mind.

When I arrived at the door, I knocked gently. The door opened, and I started to speak when the man said, "I am sure glad to see you." He went on to say, "You had been gone only a short time when I received a phone call from the people who rented the property. They have been transferred to another job far from the area and desperately need to cancel their rent arrangements."

By divine intervention, God had handled the arrangements so we could rent the property for the mission. He blessed us there in our years of ministry in Puerto Rico.

"He performs wonders that cannot be fathomed, miracles that cannot be counted." **(Job 5:9)** *"We must pay the most careful attention, therefore, to what we have heard, so that we do not drift away ... God also testified to it by signs, wonders and various miracles."* **(Hebrews 2:1–4)** *"You are the God who performs miracles; you display your power among the peoples."* **(Psalm 77:14)**

25

Kindness of a Haitian Grandmother

"Therefore, as God's chosen people, holy and dearly loved, clothe yourselves with compassion, kindness, humility, gentleness and patience." **Colossians 3:12**

Mary and I had been invited to join a work team for a project in Haiti. On arrival in Haiti, the team was anxious to begin the assignments. Many sponsored children were to be visited to see how their progress was taking place. We also had construction projects. Work teams had become an important opportunity for service at mission projects around the world, and many people were willing to give their time to assist. Team members raised their own funds and pooled skills and resources to make each mission trip successful.

Each of our visits to the mission projects provided us the opportunity to interact with the people and culture of the country. The trips were always a blessing, and we had the opportunity to make many new friends. The intent of our work was to give to others, but often we left with memories and experiences that enhanced our journey of faith. This was the case on the trip when I met the Haitian grandmother and found new meaning to the word *kindness*.

Our first week of work was taxing. Several projects needed to be completed before we left in two weeks. The heat and humidity were high, and

Faith Journeys

it was a continual effort to stay hydrated. While the men did construction work, the women on the team traveled the back roads in an open pickup truck, checking on the needs of the children. Having worked hard all week, Mary and I and the others on the team looked forward to a day of rest and the Sunday afternoon worship service in a rural, isolated village.

The Haitian Christians were happy to have us as their guests. They prepared a meal of goat and rice for us. We graciously shared in the food they had prepared before proceeding to the church building for the service.

The church was a small, primitive structure made of thin, bark covered trees randomly laced together with a precarious rafter arrangement that allowed little head clearance upon entry. Palm leaves were carefully secured across the top to provide shade from the simmering hot sun. It was certainly a cultural experience to worship there, extremely different from the spacious, air-conditioned places of worship in the USA.

Numerous parents with many little children as well as many elderly were already present when we arrived. Big smiles greeted us, and we were quickly escorted in and given seats on the few homemade chairs available. Mary and I were willing to sit on the ground as many others would be doing or even stand as many did, but the church leaders insisted we sit on the chairs. They were so gracious, and we did not want to offend them, so we sat down.

It was not long before the building was packed from wall to wall with people. Many were standing outside looking in because there was no more room inside. Several small children crowded around my feet. The wobbly little chair I sat on barely held me. To make more room, two little children chose to sit on my lap, making room for others on the floor. I feared the rickety chair would collapse, but it held. Mary also held children on her lap.

The bright sun beat down on the little building, and it filtered through the many slits in the palm leaf roof. I felt as if I were sitting under a large, inverted, handmade basket. The high humidity, soaring heat, and hot sun along with the smallness of the building crowded with people made perspiring inevitable.

The Haitian Christians not only honored their guests with chairs, but they also provided chairs for their elderly. Sitting next to me was an elderly Haitian grandmother. She could easily have been the age of my own grandmother. Her eyes sparkled, and she had a big smile on her

Kindness of a Haitian Grandmother

face. She often turned and looked at me with a big, welcoming smile as everyone joined together in our time of worshiping the Lord.

I continually struggled to maintain my balance on my chair, juggling the two little children sitting on my knees to keep them from sliding off. To ensure that they would not fall and land on the children sitting at my feet, I held both securely with my hands. Beads of sweat formed all over me. Sunbeams racing through the small openings in the palm leaf roof bounced off my scalp. As sweat collected on my head, it began to stream down my face and drip off my chin. I tilted my head back and forth in an effort to keep it from breaking through my eyebrows and running in my eyes.

Trying to focus on the speaker, I wondered how my aching, sweating body was going to survive the lengthy service. The volume of sweat was increasing, and I knew in a matter of time it would run in my eyes. My hands were not free to react, as I needed them both to balance the little children on my knees. I braced myself for the inevitable, the burning sensation that was bound to happen when the sweat would flow in my eyes.

I believe God, in his greatness, orchestrates and directs events according to his master plan. God uses circumstances to enhance our spiritual understanding and help us in the process of our spiritual formation. I did not realize that God was preparing me for a better understanding of the meaning of kindness. I had read about the fruits of the Spirit, and I knew the definition of kindness, but the unconditional kindness I was about to receive would demonstrate a powerful lesson.

As I sat there in my dilemma, I suddenly felt a gentle hand, holding a cloth, carefully wiping the sweat from my brow. I turned and saw the dear elderly Haitian grandmother, smiling as she gently cleared the perspiration off my brow with an old rag. Tears joined the flow of sweat as I felt the love of God flowing through the hand of this dear soul. God had placed her there next to me to teach me a very important lesson.

She was a follower of Christ who, by our cultural standards, was in extreme poverty. She had nothing in the way of material goods. She lived without electricity or running water. She had no Social Security income, no health insurance. The simple wood and mud block shelter she called home had a dirt floor. She existed day to day in a state of survival, hoping and praying for the next meal. Yet she was not complaining in her poverty. She was not lamenting over her plight in life. Instead, with a big smile on her face, she was helping a total stranger.

Faith Journeys

Often, in the culture of the USA when someone makes a large donation, we gather for that important photo opportunity with everyone holding an enlarged copy of a check being given. This "photo op" gives the media something to publish for all to see and copies for us to keep. Our superficial smiles with all hands holding the check appear in the local media to verify credit of our participation and meet our social, cultural obligation of participation. After all, doing so is important to our personal image.

Certainly these donations are deeply appreciated and are an essential part of God's plan to help others, but what is our spiritual benefit from these events? In contrast, this dear Haitian sister in Christ, with nothing to gain and only wanting to give, demonstrated the love of God by her actions. She gave unconditional kindness directed by the Spirit of Christ that flowed from her heart. She helped me understand giving and caring for others that comes from the heart of a child of God.

I am sure by now that this grandmother in Christ has arrived safely in the arms of Jesus. She has earned and received her reward, while we remain in our tangled web of existence, seeking to find our way.

That day I learned unconditional kindness and concern for others from this elderly Haitian grandmother. I learned that happiness is not necessarily found in fame, fortune, or the material goods of this world. True happiness is found alone in Jesus Christ and our relationship with him.

26

A Child's Love for His Papa

"LORD, what are human beings that you care for them, mere mortals that you think of them?" **Psalm 144:3**

I had been invited to assist in a mission project in Guatemala at a mission school. I would be speaking at the high school graduation, and several ongoing construction projects were to take place as well. Every day would be filled with numerous activities. Mary and I had made several trips to Guatemala to help at the school, but for this trip, she had remained back home in Indiana. Little did I know I would encounter a life-changing demonstration of a little child's love for his papa.

At the time of the encounter, our team was in Guazacapan, Santa Rosa, which is on the southwest coast of the country. The mountains and volcanoes were behind us, and we could see the Pacific Ocean from the mission. The mission was facing a water crisis, so each person on our visiting team was given only one bucket of water for use each day for all of our needs. Hardship was a way of life for the people living here.

Years had passed. Our children were grown, and Mary and I were grandparents. My father had passed away, and my aging mother was living in a care facility near our Indiana home. I was older, but my faith journey was continuing.

Faith Journeys

Each time I would leave the country on a mission trip, I knew that if something were to happen to one of my family, getting home would be difficult. Years before I had told my grandfather good-bye, never to see him again in this life; the same had happened with my uncle, whom I also loved dearly. These two family members were precious to me. My uncle and grandfather and I had spent many hours camping and fishing in times past, and there was a strong bond between us.

Saying good-bye was a part of the life of a missionary. Saying good-bye to family at home when we left and then saying good-bye to the people we served on the mission when we left them was always difficult. We understood it was impossible to be with all our international family at one time, and we dearly loved and cared about all of our Christian friends and family around the world. This trip to Guatemala was no different, so I coped with my feelings.

After a long day of construction work at the mission school, we were scheduled for an evening service in a large church in a nearby community. When the evening meal was over, everyone began cleaning up and getting ready for the trip. We had to be ready when the van driver was ready to leave, so we rushed to prepare to go.

I had finished dressing and was hastily walking down a corridor of the school, adjusting my tie as I passed by the school office, when I heard the sound. In those days, we relied on the fax machine for international communications. The sound was the fax machine printing.

I quickly entered the office and retrieved the printout. I could hear the voices of the people as they prepared to get in the waiting van. Scanning the fax, I walked toward the van. It was from Mary. It read, "Jim, I regret to inform you that your mother has fallen and broken her hip. She is being taken to surgery at this time. The doctor has informed us that due to her age and health issues, she may not survive the surgery. We will inform you of any more news."

I was crushed emotionally. My mother was in crisis, I wanted to be by her side, but I knew it was impossible. Tears welled in my eyes as I hastily folded the faxed page and put it in my pocket. The van driver was telling everyone to gather at the van so they could load up. I knew, because of limited vehicles, that the van would be fully packed. I quickly made my way to the van, trying to brush tears from my face so as to not appear emotionally disturbed.

A Child's Love for His Papa

There was absolutely nothing I could do regarding my mother's situation. It was impossible to go to the airport and get a flight at this late hour of the day. The airport was several hours away, and communications to arrange a flight were limited. I was there in Guatemala to assist and be an encouragement to the people. I was supposed to be strong and supportive of everyone going into the service, not emotionally distraught.

My mind was in a whirlwind of emotions. I felt any moment I would break down and cry, yet I had to retain my composure and remain calm and strong. As the van pulled out, I wrestled with my grief. I am sure my demeanor was very subdued, but no one said anything.

We arrived at the church. Several steps led up to the main entrance. A couple of large, supportive columns were on each side of the entrance. Many people were already seated, and more were entering the building. I momentarily slipped away from my group and quietly stood behind one of the columns where I could not be seen. Still wrestling with my sorrow and concern for my mother who was in surgery, I kept wiping away the tears.

The uncertainty of not knowing if she would survive kept my mind wondering as I prayed for her. The possibility of never seeing her alive again entered my mind. My role for the evening service was to be a supportive presence for the local ministry. Realizing that I needed to go on into the service, I wiped my tears once again and stepped out from behind the column. God was about to teach me a lesson about commitment, compassion, and responsibility.

On the steps leading up to the church entrance, I saw a frail young man, a little boy, and two elderly Christian men. The men were on each side of the sick man, holding him because he could not stand on his own. At the sick man's feet was the little boy, who would lift the feet of the man one at a time, placing them on each step. The man had no wheelchair, and he was too weak to use crutches.

Already traumatized by my mother's dilemma, I focused as best as I could on the scene unfolding before me, willing my compassion for the man and the boy into perspective. Here I was, a strong, robust, adventurous individual who had traveled the world and faced many dangers, but I found myself feeling totally helpless. I was isolated from my mom in her crisis, and before me was a scene that tore my heart apart. I stood there, helpless, unable to do anything.

The man, with the help of his friends and the little boy, made his way into the church and took a seat. I then entered the church. The only remaining seat in the crowded sanctuary was next to the boy and the man.

God was planning every move. He had made a place for me there next to the boy to teach me a lesson about life, commitment, compassion, and service. I was to learn human suffering from a different perspective. My faith journey had led me next to this little boy. From this point, both of our journeys of faith would be impacted as we shared our mutual crises.

I love learning and have spent a lifetime in classrooms, both as a student and as a teacher, but on that day I sat quietly and silently in a crowded church building in another land. Luke 10:21 says, *"Jesus, full of joy through the Holy Spirit, said, 'I praise you, Father, Lord of heaven and earth, because you have hidden these things from the wise and learned, and revealed them to little children.'"* A little boy was about to become my instructor.

As the music began and the people sang, tears ran down the face of the suffering man. The little boy, sitting next to me, took out an old cloth and gently wiped the tears from the man's face. Assuming the little boy was the child of the man, I said in Spanish, "Tu papa?" ("Is this your father?") The little boy looked up to me and said, "Si, senor." ("Yes, sir.") My emotions continued to build, and tears welled up in my eyes.

God spoke to me. My mother, as much as I loved her and wanted to be by her side in her suffering, was very elderly and had lived a long, active life. She was ready to meet the Lord. I had to ask myself, was my emotional sorrow really pity for my not being with her?

As a young boy, Jesus said to Mary and Joseph, *"I must be about my Father's business"* (Luke 2:49 KJV). In the scene before me, I saw a young father with his small son. The boy's father was facing death from an incurable illness. My mother, too, was facing the possibility of death from her crisis. My mother had the best of medical care along with insurance to cover all costs. The father here was without medical care. He had no insurance and was dying in poverty. Here was I, a son, who was broken and in sorrow for his parent. Beside me sat a little boy in sorrow for his parent who was dying.

The Holy Spirit helped me to bring into focus what I needed to understand. I certainly had not abandoned my concern for my mother, whom I dearly loved and cared about. I knew she was in good hands. My responsibility was to be the son God called me to be, doing his business, here and now in this place.

My focus and attention turned to the little boy and his ailing father. The father wanted to go and pray at the altar at the front of the church. I assisted him along with his son and his friends. My prayers and concern poured out for them. I was a mature believer and needed to be strong and able to cope. Here was a child who would soon have to say good-bye to his father and be orphaned, not understanding why. I had an obligation to this child and his father, so I channeled all my focus to helping them in their crises.

My mother would survive her surgery and lived a few more years before passing away. This little boy's father would live a little longer also before he too passed away. Yes, in time, I would lose my mother, and the little boy was going to lose his father. But on that day, God had placed the man and his son in my life to provide an important lesson for me. He brought me to my knees to lift me up.

27

She Gave out of Her Poverty

"Jesus sat down opposite the place where the offerings were put and watched the crowd putting their money into the temple treasury. Many rich people threw in large amounts. But a poor widow came and put in two very small copper coins, worth only a few cents. Calling his disciples to him, Jesus said, 'Truly I tell you, this poor widow has put more into the treasury than all the others. They all gave out of their wealth; but she, out of her poverty, put in everything—all she had to live on.'" **Mark 12:41–44**

Mary and I had been working at the mission in Guatemala. We traveled there often to help with projects, and our Guatemalan friends always welcomed us with open arms. There was always much to do, such as painting and construction work. Now, having completed the work for this trip, we were getting ready to return home. We had finished packing and had completed our evening meal. We were preparing for the final evening service before our departure the next morning.

Guatemala has many beautiful cities, and there are many wealthy people living there. The focus of our ministry efforts, however, was the very poor Mayan Indian people living in the mountainous area. Most of the people in the area of the mission lived out in the mountains where

Faith Journeys

there were no roads. The majority did not own a vehicle. Only trails through the heavily forested area led to their homes. Church, however, was an important part of the culture of the people in Guatemala, so they faithfully attended every available service regardless of the weather and the long walk from their homes.

The local church was the center of life for the people. Activities and events took place nearly every day. On women's night, the fathers and all the children would come to be supportive when the ladies led the service. On men's night, the moms and the kids would all be there. On teen nights or children's events, the entire family would come. Regular midweek prayer and Bible study services were part of the life of the church families in addition to the weekend worship services.

During heavy rains, water would flow in the deep ditches that were at the edge of the road that passed by the mission. Water would rush into the culverts and race into the many streams that flowed through the forested, jungle terrain. It was so treacherous that one day as a mother and child attempted to cross a rain-swollen ditch near the mission, the woman's child was swept from her arms. The child was later found two miles downstream. The child had drowned.

The Sanchez family walked an average of twenty-five miles a week in order to attend services. Like most of the families in the area of the mission, there was no road to their home in the heavily forested area of the jungle. The nearest paved road was at the mission, two and a half miles away from where they lived. The family would walk the five-mile round trip to their home through the dense vegetation nearly every day of the week. The trail that led to their home opened onto the road near the mission. Before service every evening, I would look out from the mission and see the Sanchez family emerging from the forest onto the road leading to the church. After service, I would see the family disappear into the jungle of trees and vegetation.

I had come to know and love this dedicated family. They always had big smiles when I would meet them. They would shake my hand and give me a big hug. This family lived in extreme poverty compared to American standards, yet in their simple life of limited material goods, they were very happy and worked hard to maintain their home and property. They were proud of what they had. They would often invite Mary and me and the other visiting workers to come to their place for meals. On our arrival at their home, they would offer one of their few simple,

She Gave out of Her Poverty

homemade wooden chairs. They always fixed the best meal possible with their limited resources.

The father had an old, dented, metal flashlight with aged batteries in it that he would use on the trails at night. It was usually dark after services in the evening when they returned home. At the best, his flashlight would only produce a dull orange glow. After all, with an income of about fifty cents day, new batteries were not an option, even if he could find some at one of the few little shops near the mission in Guazacapan.

After services at the church in the evenings, families would remain and visit as long as possible. Church was not only a place of spiritual renewal, but it was also the social life of the people's culture. As the families slowly said their good-byes after long visits, they would drift off into the dark night to their homes.

Each night, Papa Sanchez would start out with his family following him. As they would enter the dark trail to their home, he would turn on his old flashlight. The dim, orange glow barely lit the trail in front of them because of the weak, aged batteries. At least the soft glow was enough to warn his family of any dangers such as poisonous vipers.

Since Mary and I were scheduled to leave for the capital and fly back to the USA the next day, I decided I would give Brother Sanchez my flashlight that evening at the close of the evening service. My bright red, two-dollar flashlight made of plastic had fresh batteries. It was certainly much better than what he had. I no longer needed it. There was no reason to take it home with me. I could buy all the flashlights I wanted back home.

I did not want to embarrass him by giving him a gift in front of others, so I placed it in a plastic bag. Arriving at the church early, I placed the bag under my seat. For this poor family, I thought, even the plastic bag would be treasured.

After service and the socializing time, when everyone was ready to depart for home, I quietly handed the plastic bag with my flashlight to Brother Sanchez. I felt honored I could share something with this father. My gift also triggered the emotional, "warm, fuzzy" feeling in me, thinking that I did well.

What I did not realize, in this game of "spiritual chess," was that God had set the chessboard for my checkmate. I had spent hours in classrooms and studies at the university so that I could become the best missionary possible, but God was not finished with my education. He kept

123

me in a state of continual learning. I was about to learn another lesson of faith from the people to whom he had sent me to serve.

Papa Sanchez graciously accepted the plastic bag with the gift in it for him. He smiled and thanked me, clutching the bag but not knowing what was in it. We said our good-byes and then he started out, gathering his children and looking for his wife to begin their two-and-a-half-mile journey back home.

About this time, Brother Sanchez's wife came up to me, smiling. She said she wanted to tell me good-bye too before they left on their journey down the dark trail to their home. She was unaware that I had given my flashlight to her husband. I smiled, thinking to myself, she will be happy with what I did. The family would have a nice bright light to use on the path home.

Eyes sparkling and with a big smile on her face, she reached out her hand to me. When I grasped her hand to say good-bye, she placed something in my hand and folded my fingers over it. Still smiling, she said, "We are so happy you came. We greatly enjoyed your visit and all that you do to make it possible for our kids to have a nice school to attend. I know your trip home will be a long journey, and you might get hungry on the way, so here is a little something to help you on your journey home." She smiled once more and departed, following her family to the darkened trail.

When she was out of sight, I slowly opened my hand. In it was two pesos. My eyes filled with tears. Two pesos! This mother in Christ had given me the equivalent of two days' wages. In contrast, I had given her family a two-dollar flashlight.

I never felt so small in all my life. All the lessons on tithing and stewardship I had studied had not included a humbling experience like this one. I was in spiritual checkmate. God, through this family, had taught me what giving was all about, and the final gift of the pesos was the checkmate.

This woman had stated, "Here is a little something to help you *in your journey home.*" Her statement was so true. Her gift left me with a lesson about caring and sharing that I will carry to my grave and my journey home to heaven.

So often in life, those who have the least give the most. So too, those with much often treasure the things they accumulate yet have trouble finding peace of mind and happiness. Matthew 16:26 says, "*What good will it be for someone to gain the whole world, yet forfeit their soul?*"

28

The Man under the Bridge

"He asked me, 'Son of man, do you see this?' Then he led me back to the bank of the river." **Ezekiel 47:6**

When Mary and I were working in Puerto Rico as missionaries, we would often cross a bridge into Bayamon, Puerto Rico's second largest city, when we needed to buy supplies. As in most large cities, homeless people seek shelter wherever they can find it. One day, while waiting for the traffic light to change by the bridge into the city, we observed a homeless man who had made a shelter under the bridge. His clothes were dirty and ragged. His hair was shaggy and matted. His possessions consisted of a cardboard mat and a few old cans. Trash and debris, along with scrub bushes and stubble grass, blanketed the riverbank under the bridge where he lived.

In Puerto Rico the poor who live in the barrios, areas of extreme poverty, exist at a level of poverty much below the level of the majority of the needy in the USA. This homeless man fell below the level of the poorest of his community.

Knowing that the family is a strong institution in Latin America, I had difficulty in understanding his seeming abandonment. Where was his family, his friends? I knew nothing about this man, but I saw a suffering human being. Was he simply desperate because of lack of employment? Was he mentally unstable?

My eyes briefly made contact with his. The depths of loneliness and despair into which he had fallen could be seen in his eyes. He was a broken human being. My heart went out to him. As I sat there waiting for the light to change, I wondered what his story might be, what circumstances had occurred to have him live here, in this way, what had driven him to such despair. Regardless, his dilemma ignited compassion in my heart and a call to action.

The traffic light changed, and we continued on. The image of this suffering individual was burned deep in my mind. I sensed a tugging of the Spirit of God, leading me back to the bank of the river. The Spirit within me wanted to embrace this broken person and let him know someone cared and loved him.

Feeling helpless and weak, my thoughts went to what could be done, what could be given that would make a difference in his life. How could a positive change happen in the life of this man? How could he be removed him from his despair? How could happiness be brought to his life?

God loved him regardless of his situation. Jesus died for this man even as he did for me. God's grace and mercy extended to this man regardless of his situation in life. I felt sent of God to be a conduit of his love toward this needy soul. It would take a miracle for me to create enough trust with this man to be able to lead him toward establishing a relationship with his Creator.

This man needed more than what I could provide. He definitely needed a social safety net. Material goods and money were not the only answer. As I prayed for him and asked God what I could do, it seemed there was little I could do personally but present him with a gift, a demonstration of the love of God by an act of kindness from a heart of compassion. Mary and I discussed it and determined we had an obligation to do so.

Mary and I discussed what we might possibly do. We decided one thing the man needed was new clothes. Driving by the area a few additional times, we estimated what size clothing he would need so we could determine what to buy. In my effort to help, I was focusing on a gift that *I could provide.*

The Man under the Bridge

We went to a nearby store and purchased everything we thought he needed, including pants, shirt, shoes, and socks. We picked a time when we thought he would be there, and we drove to the location. He was there, sitting under the bridge. His eyes stared off in the distance. Loneliness flooded his face. Trash littered the ground around him.

Parking the car near the bridge, Mary let me out but remained in the car with our girls. With the gifts we had for him, I climbed the guardrail and moved down the embankment toward him. I did not know the state of mind of the man nor what circumstances resulted in his being there, but I felt a need to make personal contact with him and attempt to build a relationship. It was my desire to share the love of God with him, perhaps cheer him up and give him encouragement.

Out of respect, recognizing the area under the bridge was this man's territory, I approached very slowly and cautiously, smiling and holding out my hand. He looked at me but did not say a word. What was the reason for his dilemma? What was his story? Would he be gentle? Would he be violent? Did he see me as a threat, an intruder to his area? Would he welcome me in his loneliness? There certainly would be some kind of reaction, but I was not sure what to expect.

As I approached, he slowly stood up, picked up an old rusty can, and began to move toward me. The stench of urine and body odor was repulsive. He was an abandoned, broken human that had been tossed from society. I extended my hand and spoke gently to him, telling him there was a gift I wished to give him. My heart cried out to the Lord for this man who was hurting so much. He was my brother in despair.

Fear was in his sad eyes. He made an unintelligible sound as he approached me. I was standing by a rock near the riverbank, so I carefully placed the gift of clothes on it, not wanting to frighten him or appear as a threat. Standing up from placing the clothes on the rock, I saw his arm holding the can go backward, preparing to swing. Without warning, he threw the contents of the can all over me.

Having had his territory invaded, he had taken the only action he knew to defend his small, remaining corner of the earth. I was drenched with stale urine. The stench was overwhelming.

I stepped back and apologized. I told him God loved him. He backed away, looking bewildered. I slowly turned to leave.

Faith Journeys

Climbing back up the riverbank and over the guardrail with tears welled in my eyes, I wondered what more I could have done to make a difference for this hurting human being. The pungent smell of stale urine filled the air. I climbed through the brush under the bridge into the hot sun, sweating heavily. I stunk, and I felt terrible about what had just transpired.

I could not get in the car with my family in my urine-soaked clothes, so I asked Mary to return to the store and buy clothes for me. I told her I would walk a few blocks to a service station with a restroom. We agreed she and the children would meet me there with soap, a washcloth and towel, and the clothes.

Walking along the riverbank toward the service station, I realized that in my journey of faith, God was transforming this event into a time of shaping and molding my spiritual life. A powerful message was unfolding before me. I was now like the man under the bridge. I was alone and forgotten by the world around me. I was a wrenched, stinking person who longed for people that passed by to understand my situation. I felt the loneliness as they moved as far away as they could from me. I felt the rejection.

I first was rejected by the man I sought to help, and then I was rejected by others. People did not want to be near me. It was I in need of a change of clothes. It was I who needed to be bathed and cleaned up. The man under the bridge now had a change of clothing available to him. I was now the man from under the bridge without.

As I waited for Mary to return so I could get cleaned up and change clothes, thoughts and emotions flooded over me like waves. I thought of how my own Lord and Savior had come to mankind, bringing robes of righteousness for humanity. He had paid the price for those robes of righteousness, and yet so many people rejected his gift. I thought of how he reached his arms of love toward humanity, only to have them throw the filth of their excuses for their behavior back at him. I thought of how he might have felt, rejected, as I had just been, as people moved away from me in disgust.

I was on God's potter's wheel again, being molded and shaped for his purpose. I was brought to ultimate humility, in a desperate state. This event was part of my journey of faith, transforming me in a way that has continued to burn deep in my soul.

128

The man under the bridge had received new clothing. I, too, had received something new. It was the recognition that I am here on earth as a soul in a human body. My body is only on loan to house the soul God gave me. It belongs to God alone and is subject to respond as he desires.

In the faith journey, continual choices must be made. I could have ignored the man and his need. I could have expressed anger in response to the action he took toward me. Realizing the purpose of my being in that moment was to fulfill the task God had assigned me to do, including facing rejection myself afterward, I was at peace.

The experience was humbling, and my eyes were opened to the needs of the destitute. I learned a lot from the man under the bridge. Regardless of his action toward me, sorrow and concern remained in my heart for him. In a strange way, through his actions, he had deepened my spiritual experience and my understanding of my obligations to others like him. The experience at the bridge that afternoon had been for a reason. God had assigned this man to teach me so I could learn to feel and understand poverty, abandonment, loneliness, and rejection.

What about the many others in our world who live lives of loneliness and feel rejected by the world around them? Jesus said, *"For I was hungry and you gave me something to eat, I was thirsty and you gave me something to drink, I was a stranger and you invited me in."* (Matthew 25:35)

"Whoever gives heed to instruction prospers, and blessed is the one who trusts in the LORD." **(Proverbs 16:20)** *"Apply your heart to instruction and your ears to words of knowledge."* **(Proverbs 23:12)** *"He taught them many things by using stories."* **(Mark 4:2 NIrV)**

29

Marvin

"You see that his faith and his actions were working together, and his faith was made complete by what he did." **James 2:22**

Many wonderful people have influenced my life, too many to name. Among those that stand out are a man and his wife, Edwin and Colleen, who left their home and gave up their careers in the Netherland Antilles to live among the people in the Dominican Republic. Through them I came to know Marvin, whose faith helped to shape mine.

It was by divine intervention that I met Edwin and Colleen and their family when I was among a group that arrived in Jarabacoa, Dominican Republic, to be a part of a medical team with Medical Ministries International. Arriving after dark, we were to be housed temporarily in the homes of the local people. There was no more room in the first house we were taken to, so my friend Ricardo said, "Jim, you go with this man." The man he pointed to was Edwin. He had an old truck, and Ricardo and his wife, Dianna, were on a motorbike. I trusted Ricardo, so in faith I climbed in the cab of the pickup truck with Edwin, a total stranger.

Edwin and I headed out in the dark, driving on dirt streets, and ended up in an area where the old truck could go no farther. Edwin parked the truck, and we got out. We walked off in the dark of the night down a small dirt road that ended in a path leading to the home of Ricardo and

Faith Journeys

Dianna. As we walked and talked, I could feel the presence of God's spirit in Edwin's life. The bond of brotherhood was established that evening, for we were a part of God's big family of believers.

Edwin and Colleen were working with the Literacy Evangelism International organization as missionaries. They had established a program of adult literacy, teaching reading and writing to the people in the mountains of the La Vega area of the Dominican Republic. Many people in the area previously did not have the opportunity to learn to read. Learning to read enabled them to be able to read the Bible and develop a stronger relationship with God. Through Edwin and Coleen's ministry, they had met Marvin and his family.

Colleen and Edwin worked together as a team, but Colleen took a special interest in children and adults with special needs. As a teacher from her home country, she used her educational skills to help the people in the mountainous area of the Dominican Republic. When she met Marvin and his family, she immediately established a plan to assist.

Marvin was an educated young man and wanted to learn more. He was wheelchair bound, so Colleen spent many hours tutoring him. Coleen's training included working with people with special needs. As a part of the literacy program, she went beyond her expected duties to use her skills to focus on those less fortunate. Colleen herself had been diagnosed with Parkinson's disease, but she did not let her difficulties stop her from doing all she could for others. She had strong faith in God, and she found the same in Marvin.

Marvin, a very intelligent boy and up to date on current events, was seventeen years old when we first met. His body had been wracked by Muscular Dystrophy, and the disease was already in an advanced stage. He had almost no control over his arms and legs and had difficulty holding his head up. He would strain to form words when trying to talk. Yet in his dire circumstances, he always had a smile and did not complain. He was a faithful believer in Christ, and people could feel the presence of God when they were with him.

Marvin's mother and brother faithfully cared for him the best they could. Colleen faithfully checked in on them and looked after Marvin when she could, assisting him as much as possible. Marvin's home would not qualify for a storage shed in our American culture. It was a flimsy, small, wood frame structure that was in danger of collapse. The roof leaked, and only a curtain separated the home's two tiny rooms.

Regardless of Marvin's living conditions and extreme physical disability, he continually displayed an attitude of love for others and faith in God. He seemed to accept his plight in life, and in faith continued to laugh and love and live.

In addition to tutoring Marvin, Colleen sought additional help for the family. She and her husband brought Marvin's needs to our attention, and our work team with the World Missionary Association was able to assist in making repairs to Marvin's home. Marvin wanted to share his thoughts, so since he struggled to speak, he provided lyrics to a song he created. Through Colleen's connections, Marvin's lyrics were put to music and recorded on a CD.

Our work team was in the Dominican Republic to conduct several prearranged projects. Teamed with local Christians, we were conducting Vacation Bible Schools for the children. We also had a medical team, gave eye tests, distributed reading glasses, and had a group of carpenters making benches for churches. Christine, a young woman who was a physical therapist, was one of our team members. She was familiar with Marvin's physical needs through her work experience. She designed a special tabletop for Marvin's wheel chair with a holder for a sipper cup so Marvin could drink with a straw on his own instead of having someone hold his cup. Our team of carpenters built the tabletop Christine designed.

God used Marvin to help shape and mold our lives, enabling us to be better Christians. Seeing him and his faith, how could we ever complain about anything? Our work team did all we could to help Marvin and his family.

Years later in the USA, as I was in the hospital heart center and facing serious surgery, Marvin found out about my physical crises and asked Colleen to send an email that he was praying for me. It was so humbling to know that Marvin, in his situation, was talking to God on my behalf. The news of his prayers gave strength to my faith. I felt a special peace, for I knew God was hearing Marvin's prayer.

On my list of people who have helped shape and mold my Christian faith, Marvin stands out as one who greatly influenced me. In my journey of faith, God used my interactions with Marvin to help strengthen my faith in my time of need.

The apostle Paul said, *"We sent Timothy, who is our brother and co-worker in God's service in spreading the gospel of Christ, to strengthen and encourage you in 3*" (1 Thessalonians 3:2). As Paul sent Timothy to strengthen and encourage, so God placed Marvin in my life to help me understand greater faith. The day will come when I will see Marvin in heaven with a new body, rejoicing and praising God whom he loved.

30

The Windblown Bible

"The word of the LORD came to me." **Jeremiah 1:11**

Events of divine intervention have taken place all over the world since the beginning of time. Many of these are recorded in the Bible; however, undoubtedly many uncountable events have occurred that are not recorded. Most people, if asked, will say they have seen or experienced things that cannot be explained except by divine action. Many of these anomalies fall outside of the law of probabilities and other statistical data. The story of the windblown Bible is one.

In my later years, while serving as a chaplain in my hometown, I received a call that a Hispanic family needed me. They were from out of the area, and their newborn baby had just passed away. The family was alone at the hospital and very distraught. No one who spoke Spanish was available to help them. They needed emotional and spiritual support. The hospital staff asked me to respond because I spoke Spanish.

I quickly picked up my Spanish Bible and headed to the hospital by car. It was a hot July day, and I had the air conditioner on for the ten-mile drive. Traffic was heavy, and I had several traffic lights to navigate on my route.

As I drove, I hastily leafed through my Bible to locate Matthew 19:14, in which Jesus said, *"Let the little children come to me, and do not hinder them, for the kingdom of heaven belongs to such as these."* I wanted to have the Scripture verse ready when I arrived because of the urgency of needing to help the hurting parents.

When I nearly ran a red light, I realized how foolish I was by taking such a risk. It seemed as if the Lord had reminded me, as he had done so often before, that he was in control. I abandoned my attempt to locate the Scripture verse and left my open Bible on the seat.

I continued my drive to the hospital, and as I did so, the air conditioner vent blew on the pages of the Bible, randomly flipping them back and forth. When I arrived at the hospital parking lot and turned off my car, the air conditioner stopped. The windblown, flapping pages of the Bible settled to a stop. There, directly in front of me, was the page containing Mathew 19:14, the very Scripture I had been trying to find.

Was this occurrence just by chance? I don't believe so.

Over my lifetime, I have relied on God in faith when facing difficult situations as well as with the little things. I have found that God has always been present, ready to perform divine intervention at any time. Not every outcome has been what I thought was the answer; but in time, I have seen how the hand of God was present, processing the full picture. Many events have unfolded only to demonstrate God's power and glory.

I believe this event was another demonstration of divine intervention. Why? Perhaps to enable me to be prepared to serve the people I was called to help, or maybe to just strengthen my faith. It did both. It also presented the opportunity to share this story for others' encouragement.

31

The Flat Tire

"And we know that in all things God works for the good of those who love him, who have been called according to his purpose." **Romans 8:28**

Often we have the tendency to complain when everyday issues of life interfere with our schedules. In our humanity we are quick to ask why. It happened to me one day when I found the tire on my car going flat.

I needed to pick up a few items in town. When I opened the garage door, I found the tire on my car very low. I was recovering from a surgical procedure, and the doctor had placed me on a five-pound weight lifting restriction. A flat tire was the last thing I needed. Realizing I had to take immediate action because I was not going to be able to change the tire in my physical condition, I told Mary my plan. I would drive the car quickly to the tire shop about ten miles north of us. I knew I was taking a chance, but I felt I could make it before the tire was completely flat.

The last thought to enter my mind was that in God's great plan of managing the affairs of his creation, he had set the time for my tire to go down for his divine purpose. I understood that people often mistake God's purpose by thinking all events must focus on their physical well-being and comfort zones. God's focus, I knew, is spiritual and eternal. So

Faith Journeys

my inconvenience of having a flat tire, I reasoned, could be a part of a spiritual purpose.

I jumped in the car and headed for the tire center, hoping I could make it before the tire lost all of its air. Driving as quickly as I could, I approached the tire shop on the left. I turned on my left turn signal, and my cell phone rang as I waited for traffic to clear. It was the secretary from the church next door to the tire center calling.

"Jim, where are you, and are you available? I really need your help." She went on to explain that a Spanish speaking person had stopped in and needed help. No one at the office spoke Spanish. "How soon do you think you can come help us?" she asked. I told her I would be right there.

I drove into the tire center. The people there knew me. I handed the keys to them and explained about the tire. I also explained about the call and said I would be back in a while. I then walked out the door and straight into the office of the church.

The secretary acted surprised because she knew I lived ten miles away. "How did you get here so quickly?" she asked. I explained. *"In all things God works for the good of those who love him, who have been called according to his purpose"* (Romans 8:28). God knew the need, so he had placed me at the door of the church, in his time and for his purpose.

We are instructed in Proverbs 3:5–6 (KJV), *"Trust in the Lord with all thine heart; and lean not unto thine own understanding. In all thy ways acknowledge him, and he shall direct thy paths."* When we live a life with reliance on the leadership of the Spirit of God, God will be revealed in many unusual ways.

32

Haggai Experience

"'From this day on, from this twenty-fourth day of the ninth month, give careful thought to the day when the foundation of the LORD's temple was laid. Give careful thought: Is there yet any seed left in the barn? ... 'From this day on I will bless you.'" **Haggai 2:18–19**

Over the years my journey of faith entered a time where it became necessary to slow the pace of my activity. Mary and I had returned to the USA and remained active in the local church. Our children were grown. Our lives were filled with many wonderful memories of living and working with the people we loved around the world.

With a life already filled with adventure and oftentimes danger, we were ready to turn our attention to other areas of service. For the last several years, Mary and I had focused our energies on organizing and taking teams on mission trips, but time was taking its toll on my health. I had nearly lost a leg in a freak accident, and I found I had developed the same genetic heart issues that had taken my father's life. Still Mary and I continued traveling and working at missions in Latin America and Africa between my hospital stays.

At one time following a complicated heart procedure, Mary was with me in the hospital room when I began talking to someone she did not

Faith Journeys

see. I said, "I can't leave at this time. I have too much to do." Mary asked to whom I was talking, and I explained that I was talking to the one standing in the doorway of my room. I was being told it was time to go. I was being taken somewhere. She explained that there was no one in the doorway.

I remain convinced to this day that I saw and heard someone there. I share this experience and offer no explanation to this event except to say it was certainly real at the time.

One heart procedure seemed to lead to other crises. I had four blockages in my heart. My heart rate dropped to such a level that a pacemaker had to be installed. Once I experienced an acute episode of pericarditis as well as serious arrhythmia issues that required several procedures. I had issues with blood clots in my legs and episodes of cellulitis in my arm with the infection moving toward my pacemaker.

Regardless of the seeming endless health crises, I was determined to continue in my ministry efforts as long as I could. I traveled internationally between crises. I had goals I wanted to see reached for the ministry in Africa. I felt compelled to continue the efforts begun in Latin America. I was doing everything possible to transfer as much of my responsibilities as director of the small missionary organization we served to someone else. Feeling my time was limited, I was preparing for whatever the Lord wanted in my life.

Life was becoming more and more difficult for me. Attacks of arrhythmia were worsening, even with medication. I had already gone through one procedure to correct the problem, but it failed to resolve the issue. I had also learned that I had developed a couple of aneurysms. My doctor at the vascular institute was concerned about my arrhythmia and possible blood clots that could lead to a stroke. I was taking blood thinners to help prevent it from happening.

At age sixty-eight, I had reached the place where I had to radically limit my physical activity. I suffered from heart issues daily. My heart was out of rhythm almost continually, and I experienced swings from a very slow heart rate to extreme high rates.

During this trying time in my life, I was reading the book of Haggai. The prophet was dealing with the problems of the Hebrew people and the destruction of the temple. He was concerned about the temple being rebuilt. What Haggai had written over two thousand years ago applied to events of that time; however, God often directs his followers to places in his Word that can be applied to their lives. I did not immediately recognize that God was using this historical book to speak to me, but he was.

Haggai 2:18–19 says, *"From this day on, from this twenty-fourth day of the ninth month, give careful thought to the day when the foundation of the Lord's temple was laid. Give careful thought: Is there yet any seed left in the barn? Until now, the vine and the fig tree, the pomegranate and the olive tree have not borne fruit. 'From this day on I will bless you.'"*

Sections in that Scripture seemed to jump out at me. I was lamenting over my inability to do what I felt I needed to do in my ministry efforts. When I read, *"Is there yet any seed left in the barn?"* (verse 19), I began to question if I would be able to continue to sow the seed of the Word of God. I questioned if my time of service was over.

As Haggai talked about rebuilding the temple, my thoughts went to the analogy of our physical bodies as the temple of God. My body certainly needed rebuilding. I read the section of the Scripture, *"Give careful thought to the day when the foundation of the LORD's temple was laid."* (verse 18). The words *"give careful thought"* came into focus for me when I thought about how I had nearly died when I was born but my father had asked God to spare my life for God's service.

I had been in and out of the heart center as a patient several times and had been informed by my heart doctors that they would try one more time to see if they could correct my chronic arrhythmia. I had become nearly immobile, with very limited activity. The doctors put me on a waiting list and said they would call me when they could schedule the procedure they needed to do.

The thoughts about my body, the temple of the Lord needing to be rebuilt, kept going through my mind. I was concerned about being able to continue working for the Lord. *"Is there yet any seed left in the barn?"*

I was sitting in my recliner at home when the phone rang with a call from the heart center. A date had been set for my surgery, September 24. My thoughts returned immediately to the Haggai passage. *"From this day on, from this twenty-fourth day of the ninth month, give careful thought to the day when the foundation of the LORD's temple was laid. Give careful thought: Is there yet any seed left in the barn? ... 'From this day on I will bless you.'"* (Haggai 2:18–19)

The scheduling department at the heart center did not know about my spiritual struggle, yet they had selected the *twenty-fourth day* of the *ninth month* for the procedure. God had spoken once again to me on my faith journey. On September 24, I arrived at the heart center with complete peace of mind that God was orchestrating the events. My "temple" was rebuilt that day, and I was taken off all heart medicine.

I have traveled internationally since then, continuing to work with the World Missionary Association on our mission's projects. God has extended my time to be able to serve a little longer. At seventy-four, I am still traveling internationally and sharing my faith. My journey of faith has allowed me to be able to interact with many wonderful people, sharing what I had to give and learning from others. I thank God daily for the added opportunity to continue my journey of faith.

Photo Gallery

Our first little band of twenty-one believers in Maun, Botswana, met out in the open under a Mopane tree. We believed in faith the ministry would reach many for Christ.

Our first reed church with a grass roof and a mud block wall front. The room on the back right is where the "cobra came to church."

Faith Journeys

Next to the shade tree and our brush arbor, the people build their first church building. The congregation grew as the people shared their faith with others. Today several congregations exist in and around the area.

The children of Maun brought a blind man to the church service one Sunday morning.

Photo Gallery

Photo taken while eating lunch along the Thamalakane River on the way to conduct services in one of the distant villages. Left to right: Jim, Mary, Gloria, Festus, and Kevin. Sara is in the baby basket with the blanket, and Sally is on the right.

In faith, we sailed for Africa in 1962. In the bottom of the ship, God placed a book that led us down the road south to the people of Botswana.

Author Biography

From his childhood days, Jim has felt a compassion for others who found life difficult. He experienced complex health issues as a child. In his teens, he shared his faith in God with migrant workers who were living in poverty. Over the years, Jim and his wife, Mary, have traveled extensively, sharing the gospel of Christ with others. He and his wife, an elementary school teacher, have lived and worked among people of Africa and Latin America.

Jim is an ordained minister with the Church of God, both in the USA and Canada. His education and training include studies at Indiana University, community colleges, and Mid-American Christian University. He accomplished numerous certifications as well at the National Fire Academy in Maryland and served as an assistant fire chief, chief fire investigator, and building commissioner. He has taught industrial arts and other vocational courses as well as courses for Ivy Tech Community College.

In addition to missionary ministry, Jim has served in chaplain ministry as well at emergency medical services. Jim presently serves as a volunteer chaplain at the Henry County Indiana Hospital. His writings have appeared in the Christian Faith column of the *Courier-Times* of New Castle, Indiana.

An adventurous and spirited person, Jim faces his challenges in faith. A devout believer in Christ, Jim believes that as long as God has a purpose for his presence, that his faith can sustain him in the face of all crises. As a survivor of numerous dangerous situations in life, Jim continues to faithfully reach out in ministry to others less fortunate.

World Missionary Association

The World Missionary Association (WMA) exists to provide spiritual, physical, and educational assistance to people around the world who are in need. The focus is to help those persons, less advantaged because of socioeconomic factors, and serve in enabling them to develop a spiritual relationship with God.

Vision Statement

The vision of the World Missionary Association is to provide programs and projects that will bring spiritual help, physical help, and educational opportunities to people around the world who have not had the opportunities or means to find assistance on their own. These goals will be achieved by missionaries from the organization traveling to the areas in need to provide assistance and by sponsoring and supporting National Christian leaders to achieve the goals of the organization.

The World Missionary Association also participates in liaison projects with other organizations with like vision to achieve its goals. The end result of its goals is to train Christian leaders and plant churches; provide medical assistance by supporting teams of trained personnel to assist clinics staffed by National trained personnel; and build educational facilities and support the necessary educational staff. The WMA networks with several other like ministries to provide medical and educational supplies and to provide team members for those ministries as well.

History

The World Missionary Association has its roots in the teachings of D. S. Warner and shares the history of the Church of God located at Anderson, Indiana. The WMA is a self-governing organization with its own board of directors. It is registered with Guide Star and can be found on their

Faith Journeys

National Directory of Non-Profit Organizations. It is also recognized as a Freestanding Organization of the Church of God. It was founded in 1963 as a support ministry for missions and missionaries around the world.

Jim Nipp has served as Director of the WMA since 1992. Members of the WMA staff have visited and assisted missions in Mexico, Honduras, Belize, Guatemala, Costa Rica, Argentina, Brazil, Bahamas, Haiti, Dominican Republic, Puerto Rico, Cuba, Russia, China, Tanzania, Botswana, and Kenya as well as other countries over the years.

The World Missionary Association has supplied work teams, staffing, and equipment to missions over the years. A long-term project in the Republic of Botswana, Africa, resulted in the establishment of the Botswana Church of God Mission with several congregations in the country today. The WMA has assisted with an elementary school project in Guatemala, supplying finances, supplies and equipment, and construction labor. The WMA has participated in medical team projects in the Dominican Republic by working with Medical Ministries International. The WMA has assisted missions in Haiti.

More information on the World Missionary Association can be found on its Web site at www.wmamissions.net.

Made in the USA
Charleston, SC
18 September 2013